T0287169

IMAGES
of America

ITALIANS IN THE PACIFIC NORTHWEST

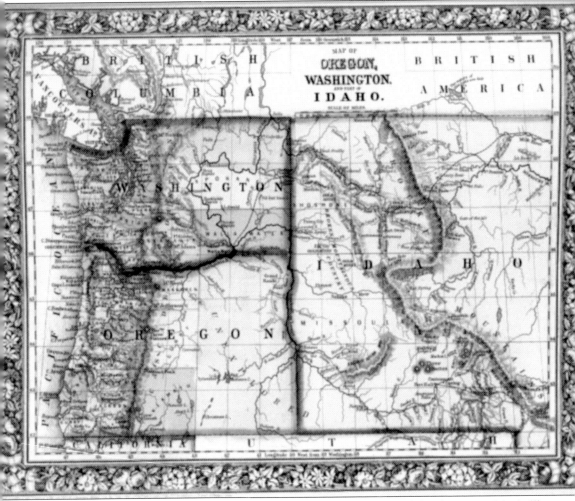

This 1863 map depicts Oregon, Washington Territory, and parts of Idaho. (Courtesy Mitchell's New General Atlas, New York Public Library Digital Collections.)

ON THE COVER: Leaving behind a wife and four children, Francesco Buono emigrated from the Bari region to the United States in 1914. He soon went from laboring as a highly skilled woodworker to running F. Buono Cabinet and Carpentry Works for 43 years. World War I prevented the family from reuniting until 1921, when Francesco's brother sailed over with the children, with Frank's wife eventually joining them in 1935. (Courtesy Frank Buono.)

IMAGES
of America

ITALIANS IN THE PACIFIC NORTHWEST

Tessa Floreano

ARCADIA
PUBLISHING

Published by Arcadia Publishing
Charleston, South Carolina

Printed in the United States of America

Library of Congress Control Number: 2023944339

For all general information, please contact Arcadia Publishing:
Telephone 843-853-2070
Fax 843-853-0044
E-mail sales@arcadiapublishing.com

Visit us on the Internet at www.arcadiapublishing.com

To the Pacific Northwest arditi, *"the Daring Ones," who dared traverse sea and land to forge forth to terra incognita—stomachs empty, hearts hopeful*

CONTENTS

ACKNOWLEDGMENTS

La gratitudine è la memoria del cuore. I am indebted to many individuals and organizations, not all of whom could be included here.

First is my family. They have given me an unending love for my deep roots in the boot, particularly the Friuli-Venezia Giulia region—from which my parents and all four sets of my grandparents hail—back to the 1600s (and counting!).

Special thanks go to Mercedes Loprinzi, Christopher Alfieri, Maia Santell, and Joe Salle. They were instrumental in helping me meet so many people willing to share their memories and photographs. In the Portland and Seattle areas, I wish to thank the following people and organizations: Jan Schoen, the Loprinzi family, Georgene Raab, Dean Chiotti, Barbara Porco, Joanna Ceciliani, Flavia Bessich, Marilyn Gatto, Greg Zancanella, Tina Jarvis, Mike Kendig, Virginia Cettolin, Tony Chiodo Sr., Sylvia Croce Zappoli, Frank Buono, Fred Marra, John Bianchi, Therese Bianchi, Tom Monahan, the Vacca family, Lisa Ursino, Ronnie Beyersdorf, Casa Italiana, Oregon Historical Society, White River Valley Museum, Rainier Valley Historical Society, Archdiocese of Portland, Black Diamond Historical Society, Museum of History and Industry, Tacoma Public Library, Granite Falls Historical Society, Renton History Museum, University of Washington, City of Portland, Whitman College, Washington State Archives, and the City of Seattle. In Idaho, the Priest Lake Museum, Museum of North Idaho, University of Idaho, and Rayna Valentine in Pocatello deserve thanks.

A special thank-you goes to my editor, Caitrin Cunningham, for her patience, as well as to Erin Vosgien, for her early encouragement, and to all the staff at Arcadia Publishing.

You hold in your hands a pictorial narrative of the ordinary—and some extraordinary—Italians who helped make the Pacific Northwest, and this nation, great. However, it would be remiss of the author not to mention that Indigenous Peoples, as well as Asian and African Americans, were never accorded the same access to jobs, opportunities, and resources that the mass arrival of European settlers had between 1880 and 1950. The social, economic, and legal hurdles these groups of people faced were not on par with the disadvantages borne by European newcomers. Though a padrone system of indentured servitude did exist, Italian laborers who participated in it could eventually drop the shackles—an affordance not as readily available to those to whom land ownership/tenancy and freedom from genocide, desegregation, racial discrimination, and criminalization was only a pipe dream. Like all countries, we have a turbulent past; however, we've hopefully learned and are still learning how to do and be better.

INTRODUCTION

The honor of the first Italian to venture into the waters of the Pacific Northwest belongs to Alessandro Malaspina, a then-37-year-old Tuscan nobleman who, in 1789, sailed for the Spanish Crown. From Cadiz to Panama, his ship followed the coastline of the Western United States up to Alaska, then onwards to the Philippines and the Antipodes. In the summer of 1791, the focus of his scientific exploration changed to finding, but unsuccessfully mapping, the elusive Northwest Passage. It was, in part, the reason the expedition did not make landfall in the Pacific Northwest.

The Pacific coast and the Northwest was the last region of the continent that Europeans explored. It proved to be full of great hardship and promise for many, as evidenced by the Corps of Discovery, the Oregon Trail, and later, the intrepid Italian immigrants of the late 19th and early 20th centuries.

Immigration before the American Civil War had been sporadic—about 25,000—and mainly favored Northern Italians, who were mostly artisans, the professional classes, and the military. Later, when those of Southern Italian origin sought to escape their mostly agrarian upbringing with the hope that their industriousness would garner them economic security, a trickle became a torrent. Eventually, over 4 million people left behind the environmental degradation caused by years of agricultural misuse, earthquakes, drought, deforestation, and bad harvests. Adding to these physical woes were the social policies of a feudal-minded aristocracy and an industrial system managed by an inept government that was unable to provide its suffering citizens effective solutions. Despite the lofty ideals of unification promulgated by the Northern reformers of the Risorgimento for a united peninsula, the mainly peasant populace of the Mezzogiorno was left, ultimately, without optimism.

Psychologically, Italians were unprepared for the effects of the new government under a single weak monarchy. Heavy taxes on top of an already dismal fiscal situation further repressed the dreams of independence that the Risorgimento or "rising again" had promised. It was not long before the verdant, expansive shores of the Americas shone like a welcoming beacon, promising the abundance and opportunity they so desperately sought. The Southern Italians eagerly awaited the reports of the first immigrants who had set out for the Americas. These unknowing scouts helped convince their families that through hard work and perseverance, the conditions on the American continents not only offered them an improved chance of surviving but perhaps thriving, too.

And thrive they eventually did, but not before facing another set of obstacles. Firstly, they experienced these obstacles at their port of entry and the crowded Eastern Seaboard, specifically New York and Boston, as well as New Orleans. Later, they endured backbreaking labor to build the iron and blacktop infrastructure needed to join this massive new land, log and mill the copious cedar sentinels that blanketed the forests of the Northwest to house others like themselves, mine the coal to heat those houses, and farm the soil and fish the plentiful waterways to feed their growing and hungry families.

While some Italian immigrants stayed in those industries, others ventured into small businesses— be they barbers, cobblers, blacksmiths, farmers, produce sellers, grocers, butchers, sausage makers, tailors, pharmacists, restaurateurs, architects, bakers, garbage collectors, construction company owners, teachers, vaudevillians, musicians, and newspapermen. From there, many grew to medium-sized businesses known locally, regionally, and nationally today.

This book tells the stories of those pioneering Italians—the trials, the triumphs, and everything in between—and perhaps a trace of Malaspina descendants in Seattle itself.

Unlike family or friends on the East Coast, those early Italians on the West Coast did not travel back to Italy very much or at all. Some wanted to forget their hardships and never set eyes on them again. Others knew saying goodbye to family twice was too much to bear. Still others made the trip, but voyages were expensive and therefore rare. There were four main factors that spurred travel back to Italy. Often, the first was to secure a wife or to help a family left behind travel to the new country *insieme*. The second was if a family member was sick or dying. The third was to fight for the homeland when war broke out in Europe. The fourth was those men, and sometimes their families, had only come to America for economic reasons, and once they had saved a decent nest egg, they wanted to return and build a home and family on their native soil.

Most of these factors were reason enough why a great number of early Italians chose not to attain American citizenship. Both world wars affected that thinking. Most were glad they were not conscripted into the Italian military, though fearing they might be called back, they quickly began the application process in order to stay in America or, for some, show their patriotism and volunteer for the US armed forces.

After World War I and the stock market crash of 1929, when the United States plunged into severe hardship and Italian men lost their jobs, they questioned whether they had made the right choice to leave their native land. Prejudice had already run rampant, making finding work in certain industries extremely difficult, but Italy's entry into World War II on the side of the Axis powers cast deeper suspicion among companies looking to hire workers or rooming houses with rooms to let.

Some Italians in Seattle and Portland found themselves squatting in Hoovervilles. These were shantytowns that had built up outside large cities across the United States. When jobs were scarce, and workers defaulted on their mortgages or were kicked out as tenants when promises to pay rent in arrears were not honored, they ended up homeless and congregated with others in the same boat. Pres. Franklin Roosevelt's New Deal was a sliver of hope that began to turn the tide, not just for Italians but for all Americans. The creation of the Civilian Conservation Corps and public works under the aegis of the Works Progress Administration provided relief to many Italians who were out of work and standing in breadlines.

As the fortunes and aspirations of all Americans began to improve when jobs were plentiful again, especially once the United States entered World War II, the hope that many Italians had given up in Italy after the Risorgimento, and again during the Depression, flickered brightly once more.

One

CHARTING A COURSE

The spirit of exploration did not die with Alessandro Malaspina or the many other Italian explorers who navigated America's shores. It lived on in the undaunted wave of immigrants—past the burgeoning urban industrial centers and into the semirural and remote enclaves of this nation, including the evergreen Northwest. Economics was certainly a driver, but so, too, was the enticement of land. Land meant wealth—possibly even generational wealth—a concept unheard of in Italy, the "old country."

From the 1880s until the early 1920s, copious labor agents in the many disadvantaged villages and towns of Italy, as well as the labor bureaus of the Americas, strongly influenced those seeking escape and new opportunity. Many immigrants bypassed lengthy stays on the East Coast and headed west, eager for ready work. The region drew these men in droves and later their families and new brides, who braved the seas and paved the way for their friends and other family members to immigrate. In the rugged wilderness, they had a chance of making it. But first, they had to bear the burden of scrutiny at their disembarkation point.

Once immigrants landed on Ellis Island, they were subjected to stringent and often intrusive physical and mental examination. They stood in long, loud, and crowded queues—breathing in stale air, ignoring their grumbling stomachs, and listening to a cacophony of 20-plus languages and dialects competing for attention.

Many Italians had a family member or a labor agent waiting for them on the mainland. Others faced a blank slate and relied on mutual aid organizations. There was a common pattern of chain migrations among immigrants, including Italians, who followed relatives to the Americas and ended up clustering together in places where they found work.

Of the thousands who headed west, who either applied for a homestead plot or purchased a home, they did so sometimes decades before their Eastern brethren. Taking the homestead route, they were in community with other Italians, could purchase what they needed, and hopefully could get on the power grid. At the labor camps or company towns, housing was provided, and it was one less thing they had to figure out on their own. If they pounded an unbeaten path as a laborer or small business owner in a city like Spokane, Portland, and Seattle, or frontier towns like Aberdeen, Astoria, and Coeur d'Alene, they took up residence in boardinghouses.

Unfortunately, over time, the steady stream of immigrants fostered a national anti-Italian sentiment among this land's citizenry. Americans of Northern European descent felt threatened and did not think Italians could assimilate. Italians were baited in public, disdained as undesirable, and refused jobs, but they persisted, facing prejudice head-on as they went.

Unsuccessful though Spain's aspirations in this area were, Malaspina's name lives on in a pristine strait and mountainous peninsula named after him near Vancouver Island. British Columbia celebrated the bicentennial of his voyage of discovery with a 1991 commemorative coin. (Courtesy Maritime Museum of British Columbia, Victoria, British Columbia.)

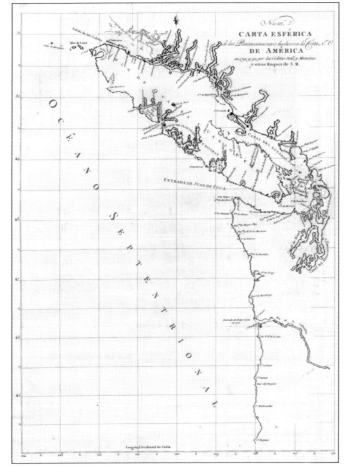

The double-headed arrow above the Canal de Rosario on this 1802 Spanish map depicts the Malaspina Strait in British Columbia. (Courtesy David Rumsey Map Collection, Stanford Libraries.)

Built in 1899 for a French steamship line, *La Lorraine*'s home port was Le Havre. Most Northern Italians departed from either Genoa or Le Havre on ships like this. The author's paternal grandfather sailed *La Lorraine* from Le Havre to New York City on May 10, 1914, two months before World War I broke out. (Courtesy Bains News Service, Library of Congress.)

The wait to see an immigration officer often felt interminable, and that was after they had passed several physical and mental health inspections. Immigrants were segregated in the registry room, but at least there were interpreters who could help them answer the officer's questions. (Courtesy ID b12326658, New York Public Library.)

Once they were cleared for landed residency status, immigrants left the main building and headed for the ferry dock, where a ferry took them across New York Harbor to Battery Park. (Both, courtesy ID 201246347, Underwood & Underwood, Library of Congress.)

Two

THE FIRST YEARS

Tilling the soil was where many Italian immigrants started in the Pacific Northwest, and soon, their fields produced enough that they could set up on their own without being victims of anti-immigrant policies. The gardeners took the fruits of their labor and sold, stored, and shared it. Jars packed to the rim with orchard fruits and row veggies were three- or four-deep on the shelves that lined their cantina walls. They made for a colorful array of "arte de giardinieri," as some *nonnas* ("grandmothers") liked to say. The cantinas, with bustling sounds and smells, were often the heart of the home. These basement kitchens were where the family ate, leaving the upstairs kitchen and dining room for company.

Those immigrants who did not garden full time showed up at a physically demanding worksite to dig ditches or coal, cut timber, construct roads and houses, or lay sewer pipe or railway track for a grueling 10- or 12-hour day. Others who were able to find less-intensive work, such as in a factory, retail store, or an office, faced obstacles related to nativism and suspicions cast over Italian allegiance to the Roman Catholic Church. Italians also had to endure constant repetition of negative portrayals in the newspapers they read when they were taking a break at work and trying to catch up on the news.

As the 19th century turned into the 20th, blatant bias and ethnic slurs in advertisements against hiring Italians for jobs was rampant and would never pass muster now. "Help Wanted, No Italians" signs proliferated shop windows, utility poles, and bulletin boards at labor centers and immigrant-rich neighborhoods.

The implementation of the Johnson-Reed Act of 1924, which set quotas on immigrants from Eastern and Southern Europe, only fueled the scorn of rising supporters of eugenics and nativism. A provisional system based on "national origin," the act permanently limited the number of these immigrants admitted into the United States to two percent per year to prevent "a stream of alien blood," as declared by the author of the act and a Republican representative from Washington State.

Ever resourceful and hardworking, Italian men looked for different solutions. The fraternal organizations and mutual aid societies that initially helped them in the early days of their American adventure were once again instrumental in giving a hand up to those who had the initiative to start their own businesses.

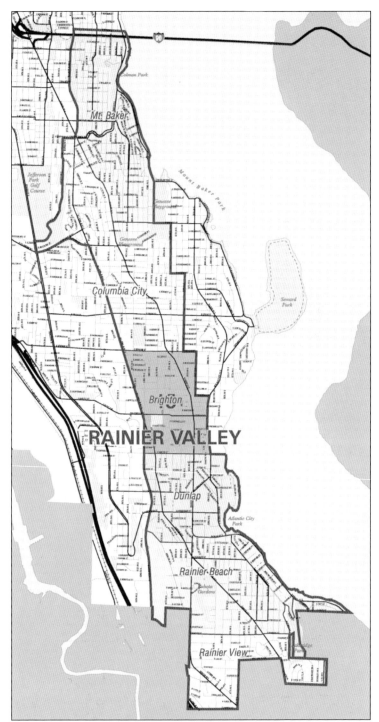

Early Italians settled in the Rainier Valley area, affectionately known by some as Garlic Gulch, bordered on the west by the Duwamish Waterway and on the east by Lake Washington. The intersection of Rainier Avenue and Atlantic Street was the main thoroughfare, and many businesses were centered near there. (Courtesy City of Seattle.)

The Jackson Hotel in Pioneer Square was run by a number of Italians, including Simon Trabucco and Stefano Raggio in 1893 and 1900, respectively. Through the early years of Prohibition, the hotel's Columbus Saloon was run by John Cicoria and John Garbarino and was a popular watering hole with members of the Italian colony at the time. (Courtesy Washington State Archives.)

In the 1920s, the Giaccarrinis lived and worked in the Rainier Valley, and like other early settlers, they labored for many years in the coal mining industry. (Courtesy Casa Italiana.)

On Christmas Day 1909 in the Rainier Valley, the Bulgarelli and Gualtieri family celebrated the holiday and gathered round for a group photograph. (Courtesy Carrie Bergquist.)

In the late 1880s and into the 1920s, Italian families like the Caveleros, Columbuses, Riccis, and Spadas farmed in Snohomish County north of Seattle, with some of their descendants serving in the US military in World War I. Dominic Cavelero was an intrepid businessman and was well known in the area to the point of having a landmark, Cavelero's Corner, named for him. (Courtesy Granite Falls Historical Society.)

Fausto Cettolin worked long days at the Bethlehem Steel Mill in West Seattle, and he and his wife, Erma, raised six children. Between 1926 and 1939, and without blueprints or any outside help, Fausto built a gorgeous Italian villa-style home and garden. When Erma was bedridden because of cancer, Fausto designed a star-shaped flower bed that she could view from her window. The Cettolin house is a historic testament to the community at large of remarkable craftsmanship that evokes a slice of Italian culture and adds a unique character to the neighborhood. The Seattle Landmarks Preservation Board has agreed to consider landmark status for this one-of-a-kind house, despite a planned light rail project threatening its preservation. (Both, courtesy Virginia Cettolin.)

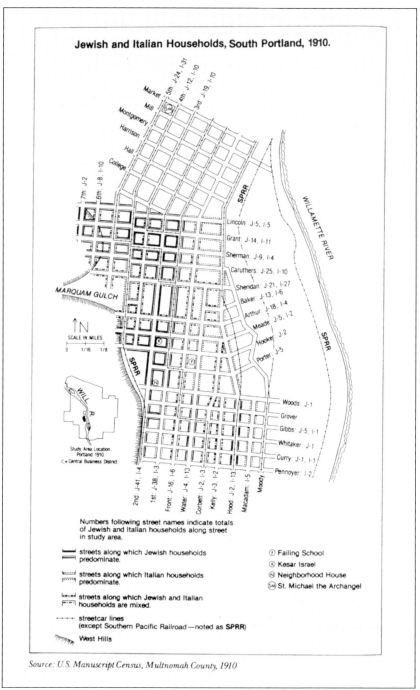

Jewish and Italian Households, South Portland, 1910.

Numbers following street names indicate totals of Jewish and Italian households along street in study area.

—— streets along which Jewish households predominate.

···· streets along which Italian households predominate.

···· streets along which Jewish and Italian households are mixed.

·+· streetcar lines (except Southern Pacific Railroad—noted as SPRR)

西山 West Hills

Ⓕ Failing School
Ⓚ Kesar Israel
Ⓝ Neighborhood House
Ⓢᴹ St. Michael the Archangel

Source: U.S. Manuscript Census, Multnomah County, 1910

Italian immigrants and Eastern Europeans of Jewish ancestry arrived in Portland around 1900, both settling into the Marquam Gulch area south of the city, near the city dump, because that is what they could afford. They established businesses, sent their children to local schools, and signed up for English classes at the neighborhood settlement house. Women learned to cook and sew there, and some were even tutored to prepare for their citizenship tests. (Courtesy US Manuscript Census, Multnomah County.)

Pictured are typical immigrant homes in the 1900s Marquam Gulch. When this became the South Auditorium renewal area, land was cleared for the new I-5 freeway. Many Italians were displaced, and the area's Little Italy was mostly lost. (Both, courtesy City of Portland Archives.)

The Duniway Park area, pictured above, was the former Marquam Gulch. Most Italians stayed in the gulch for a couple of decades. Some saved enough to buy land, build a home, and establish truck farms east of the Willamette River near the newly platted Ladd's Addition. Yet others stayed until they were forced to move. (Both, courtesy City of Portland Archives.)

Bakers since 1687 in Pagno, Italy, the Chiottis arrived in Portland in 1903 and opened several bakeries, including Alessio's in 2003, started by Dean Chiotti, great-grandson to the founder, Ambrogio Chiotti (bottom row, far left). (Courtesy Dean Chiotti.)

Pictured are early settlers and produce sellers in Portland. They are, from left to right, (first row) George Bocci, Jeanne Catanese, and Catherine Greco Corno; (second row) Joan Bocci, Josephine Greco Bocci, Rosa Loprinzi Greco, Frank Corno (of Corno's Produce), Lena Greco Catanese, and Joe Catanese; (third row) Frank Greco, Ruth Greco, Angelo Bocci, Giuseppi Greco, Gus Greco, and Pete Catanese. (Courtesy Jan Schoen.)

Early Seattle pioneers Luigi and Maria Grandinetti are on their front porch with their daughter, Angela Rose, enjoying some time away from their grocery store business. (Courtesy Kathy Childers.)

From 1892 to 1894, the six Naccarato brothers from Calabria arrived in Priest River, Idaho, to help build the Great Northern Railroad. From left to right, Mike, Joe, Charlie, Frank, and Tony (Angelo is missing) were the first wave of Italian immigrants and part of the first crews to make ties and build grades. Their father, Angelo, bought a 160-acre homestead, and each son built a home a year. (Courtesy Bonner County History Museum.)

BOEING PRESIDENT CLAIRE EGTVEDT HONORS JOE DESIMONE, 1937; THE FARMER GIVES HIS LAND

In 1898, Giuseppe "Joe" Desimone, an 18-year-old immigrant from Naples, managed to thrive as a farmer and produce seller in his first decade in America. He sold his vegetables at the Pike Place Market, but eventually, he bought the market in 1941, solidifying his success. From early on, there was racial and ethnic harmony, leaving the market as much a place of opportunity for many immigrants then as it is now. When Boeing was looking to move out of Seattle in the 1930s due to lack of space for an airport, Desimone sold the company some prime farmland for $1 if it agreed to stay in Seattle. And the rest, as is often said, is history. The photograph is of Joe (right) accepting an award from Clairmont Egtvedt, then president of Boeing, for the sale of his land. (Courtesy Boeing Company.)

23

Though Frank Orselli, a former soldier, is credited as the first Italian settler in Walla Walla, it was Pasquale Saturno, also known as "Frank Breen," who arrived in 1876 to become the first commercial produce gardener in the valley. He built a small house for his young family and a subsequent larger house years later. (Both, courtesy American Folk Life Center, Library of Congress.)

It was difficult for people to pronounce Pasquale Saturno's name, so over time, it changed to "Frank Breen," which came about from his selling efforts—"I breeng you onions." Besides peddling onions, he produced wine, even during Prohibition, in his cellar (below). Home winemaking, up to 200 gallons per household per year, was allowed during that time. Above is Frank on the far left at the funeral of a Saturno baby in the early 1900s. (Both, courtesy Italian Americans in the West Project Collection, American Folk Life Center, Library of Congress.)

WALLA WALLA, WASH.

DEDICATION OF COLUMBUS MONUMENT

OCTOBER 12, 1911

On October 12, 1911, the Italian colony in Walla Walla raised the funds to commission a statue to commemorate Christopher Columbus. The work represented Italian immigrants overcoming challenges and was a historical connection to their homeland. (Left, courtesy Whitman College Northwest Archives; below, courtesy Joe Drazan.)

DEDICATED TO CHRISTOPHER COLUMBUS ITALY'S ILLUSTRIOUS SON WHO GAVE TO THE WORLD A CONTINENT. WE SHALL BE INCLINED TO PRONOUNCE THE VOYAGE THAT LED THE WAY TO THIS NEW WORLD AS THE MOST EPOCH MAKING EVENT OF ALL THAT HAVE OCCURRED SINCE THE BIRTH OF CHRIST ERECTED BY HIS ADMIRING COUNTRYMEN THE 12TH DAY OF OCTOBER A. D. 1911.

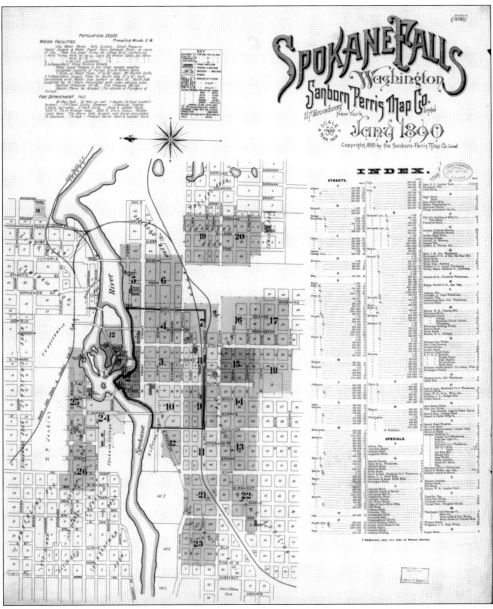

From the 1880s to 1930s, Spokane's Greek, German, Italian, Japanese, and Chinese working-class immigrants were congregated in the bustling Trent Alley (marked in dark outline). They operated small businesses like barbershops, grocery stores, pool halls, restaurants, and hotels, which attracted itinerant lumbermen, miners, railway workers, and later, families. Around World War II and after, the Italian pioneers moved into the Minnehaha, Hillyard, and Altamont neighborhoods and became produce sellers, farmers, barbers, cobblers, and restaurant owners. Well-known Italian community spaces were Mauro's Grocery, Felice Barbershop, and St. Mary's Catholic Church. (Courtesy Sanborn Maps Collection, Geography and Map Division, Library of Congress.)

Buffalo Courier.

BUFFALO, N. Y., SUNDAY MORNING, JUNE 30, 1907.

BUSINESS, WORK AND OPPORTUNITY FOR ALL

At the turn of the last century, newspapers from all over the country carried headlines eager for cheap labor (oftentimes made up by immigrants)—"Business, Work and Opportunity for All." This call can be juxtaposed with a classified advertisement (inset) from the same newspaper refusing to hire Italians in 1907. (Courtesy *Buffalo Courier*.)

Seeing an increasing need for social services for the burgeoning Italian colony in the Rainier Valley, nurse Jesse Gasser and teacher Mary Jane Hepburn from the United Methodist Church founded the Deaconess Settlement in a small house. In 1928, they moved to this purposely built brick building on Atlantic Street that still stands today serving a new generation of immigrants. (Courtesy Joe Mabel.)

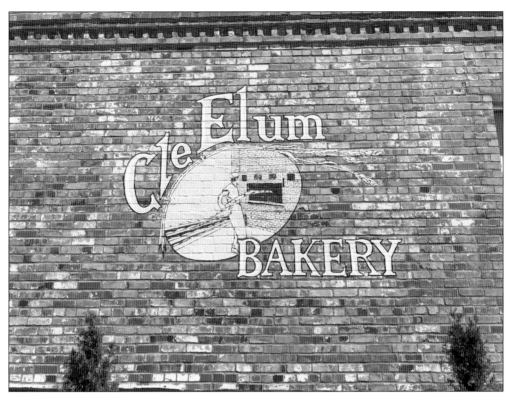

Founded in 1906 by John Pricco, Cle Elum Bakery, the oldest in Washington State, still has its original brick ovens, which have never cooled since their installation over 117 years ago! Famous for its French bread, doughnuts, and cookie varieties, the bakery is both a local and tourist destination. (Courtesy author's collection.)

Frank Buono had a cabinetmaking business, but he also dabbled in entertainment—the Star Pool Room to be exact. Card and pool tables were next to the bar, while fresh fruit, candy, and tobacco products were in display cases up front. It is hard to know what all happened in those back rooms, but the police were frequent interrupters during Prohibition. (Courtesy Frank Buono.)

Next door to Orrico's Barbershop on Rainier Avenue was Tony's Shoe Shop, and in the 1920s, it was a happening place. Both were where men congregated and caught up on life. In 1931, a Seattle directory had over 200 shoe repair shops, many of which were run by Italians. (Courtesy Maia Santell.)

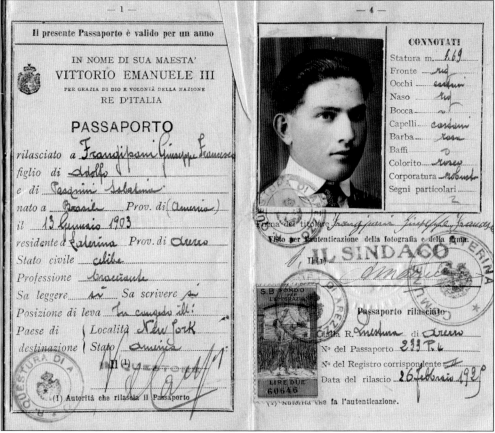

Born in Brazil, farmer Giuseppe Francesco Frangipani, of Italian descent, immigrated to Portland in the early 1920s. It is interesting to note on this example of an early Italian passport that the citizen had to identify whether they were literate. (Courtesy Marilyn Gatto.)

In 1886, Luigi Grandinetti immigrated from Parenti, near Cosenza, in Calabria. From her home in Trenta, near Cosenza, Maria Palma Cosentino followed in 1901. The family believes that it might have been an arranged marriage because Maria wed Luigi the same year. He eventually opened a grocery story on Main Street in the Pioneer Square district of Seattle. An interesting sign is seen over his left shoulder, and it reads, "Sweetheart Day April 17." In the same year that Luigi arrived, he applied for naturalization, one of the earliest records of naturalization in Washington State. (Both, courtesy Kathy Childers.)

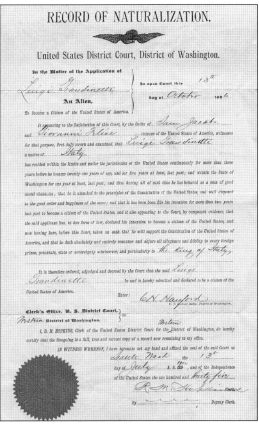

In 1880, when Salvatore Cosentino was just 23, he crossed the sea and the entire United States to head west to what was then Washington Territory. He was a resident before Washington became a state in 1889. He married Angeline Donofrio Cosentino in 1911, raised a family, and farmed in Sequim for 59 years. (Courtesy Kathy Childers.)

| 1892 | Register of Voters | First | Precinct | First | Ward |

Date of Register	Politics	NAME		Age	OCCUPATION	RESIDENCE	REMARKS
Jan. 8		Pinkus Ben.		24	Merchant	S. 2d + Wash.	changed to 3–1
11		Picardi Peter		29	Sailor	R.R. Ave. + Charles	
12		Pruner G.D.C.		42	Compositor	121 West Main	
13		Pendergast John		26	Mill hand	Comml. + Jackson	
"		Peirce S.P.J.		25	Bridge Carpenter	" + Wash	
15		Pealer M.W.	✓	35	Truckman	Near Mechanics Mill	
16		Peters N.P.		43	Cigar stand	420 Comml.	
20	R.	Peccard Henry		27	Merchant	Windsor Hotel	J
21		Pattison W.R.	✓	46	Express	505 Comml.	
22		Parker James		37	Laborer	Y.Z. Lodging House	
25		Paice D.		23	Steamboatman	Foot of Wash.	
26		Paulson Peter		33	Sailor	Babcock House	By S......

Peter Picardi, a 29-year-old sailor, is the second person listed on the 1892 Seattle Voter Roll, the first evidence of an Italian who registered to vote in the city. That year was a national election and the first one that Washington participated in as a state. This is remarkable considering only 71 Italians were included in the territorial and state censuses from 1857 to 1892. (Courtesy University of Washington Collection, Museum of History and Industry.)

Three

A Helping Hand

It did not take long for the Italian diaspora to form fraternal organizations and mutual aid societies to address such a very great need to help their countrymen. Early ones, such as the Fratellanza Society, Knights of Columbus, and the Sons of Italy, sprouted chapters all over the country and still have members' meetings a century later. These self-help groups lent a hand with assimilation, housing, health, and employment concerns, including any injuries or deaths related to one's job. Such financial assistance, including funerary, was decades before the protection of unions and workers' compensation.

These male-only clubs, along with others, such as the Italian Independent Society and the Italian Benevolent Society, excluded women until the 1930s and 1940s. A brave few, like Emilia Russo Colarossi, petitioned these organizations for the right to charter their own. In 1925 and 1927, respectively, Sorelle della Società Italiana Independente and the women-only chapter of the Ordine Figli D'Italia in America were formed. They were not only the first such groups in Seattle but the first ones in the United States. Part social clubs, part philanthropy, and later, strong participators in civil rights struggles, these organizations welcomed all women, offering support (sometimes financial), family-friendly events, and friendship.

Mutual aid also came in the form of cooperatives, which are businesses owned and governed by member-owners. They were mostly vegetable sellers like Joe Desimone who helped found Pike Place Market in Seattle, truck farmers in Portland who built their own building when they formed the Italian Gardeners and Ranchers Association, and the onion farmers in southeastern Washington who banded together to form the Walla Walla Produce Co. They pooled their capital, and the profits they generated were shared among the members.

Distrustful of banks, many Italians who were not part of co-ops but still needed loans or reliable savings safekeeping relied on local businessmen like Guido Merlino in Seattle or Garibaldi Grocery in Portland, whom many felt were safer than a bank. However, there were some banks Italians trusted, and a few examples of those are as follows: the Myers family's incorporated Italian American Bank (1906) in Portland and two in San Francisco, the Italian American Bank (1899) and the Bank of Italy (1904) by Sigg. Andrea Sbarboro and Amadeo Pietro Giannini, respectively. These men and their banks democratized banking for immigrants and helped Italians triumph in the face of ignorant bankers unwilling to loan money to "the little fellow." Much like the mutual aid societies, character and a solid handshake over meager savings and collateral was what counted at these banks, and it made all the difference.

Cartoons from *Puck*, a late-19th to early-20th century humor magazine, depicting foreigners, especially Italians, as an undesirable people were common in the early 1900s. The one above shows European rulers cheering Uncle Sam as the Pied Piper leading a swarm of rats carrying knives and ransom notes with the Black Hand insinuating the lax labor laws were admitting thieves, assassins, and other degenerates into the country. The one below shows hyphenated Americans (the first representing Italians) going to vote and Uncle Sam has his back to them. (Above, courtesy Library of Congress; below, courtesy Billy Ireland Cartoon Library & Museum, Ohio State University.)

THE HYPHENATED AMERICAN.

UNCLE SAM. — Why should I let these freaks cast whole votes when they are only half Americans?

Angelo Merlino (in the fedora), founder of Merlino Foods, an imported Italian food purveyor in Seattle, helped sponsor a local baseball team through the Italian Independent Society, a local benevolent group. (Courtesy Casa Italiana.)

Società Di Mutuo Soccorso was an Italian mutual benefit society in Seattle. Shown here in the early 1920s outside of Our Lady of Mount Virgin, the local Italian church, are the society's officers in their regalia. (Courtesy Chris Alfieri.)

Italians, like other immigrants, formed benevolent or mutual aid societies in the early 1900s not only to combat the prejudice they were subjected to but also to help fellow countrymen and women. Seattle was the foundational home to at least the following three national societies: Sorelle Della Società Italiana Independente, Ordine Figli D'Italia in America, and the Italian Club for Women. The latter was founded in 1926 by Cathenne Menga and others; it disbanded in the midst of World War II and reorganized in 1948 as the Women's Auxiliary. It was renamed the Women's Italian Club in 1999 and disbanded on January 1, 2004, when women were finally welcomed into the Italian Club of Seattle as full and equal members. (Both, courtesy Roz Mascio.)

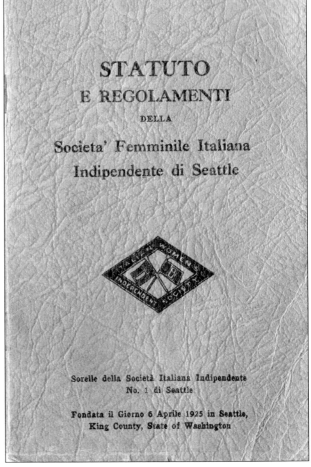

In 1952, Lucy Salle, an active member of the Italian colony in Seattle, was installed as an officer of Fedele 1469, the first female-only chapter of the Order of the Sons and Daughters of Italy in America (OSDIA), which was cofounded by her mother, Emilia Colarossi. (Both, courtesy Joe Salle and Lucy Salle.)

ARCH, 1952   LO SVEGLIARINO

eattle Lodges Install Their Officers In A Colorful Ceremony

Mrs. Lucy Salle, Venerable of Fedele Lodge No. 1469, Dr. Nicholas Sarro, Special Grand Deputy, and Louis LiCastro, Venerable of Seattle Lodge No. 1390, Order Sons of Italy, are pictured above as the rand Deputy presents the two Venerables the Gavels of their office.

The Installation was held Sunday, March 16 at the Casa Italiana, 7:30 p.m., following a Spaghetti inner served to all those present. Among the Grand Officers present were: Rudolph Naccarato, Grand enerable; Frank Orrico, Assistant Grand Venerable; Frank J. Carbone, Ex Grand Venerable; Nick oselli, Act. Grand Recording Secretary; Frank Costi, Grand Financial Secretary; John Demattea, rand Treasurer, and John Anthony, Grand Trustee.

Also present were: Nick Maffeo, Venerable Renton Lodge; Pete Santoro, Venerable Colombo Lodge; e Palladini, Venerable Portland Lodge; Joe Lupo, Venerable Tacoma Lodge; Louis Riconoscluto, en. elected of Tacoma Lodge, Mrs. Afien Lupo, Ven. Elected of Virtus Lodge; Joe Pezzella, from uburn Lodge and many more visitors from our neighboring cities.   Photo by (Walters Studio).

Pictured is a gathering in 1949 of the Italian American Progressive Club in Tacoma, Washington, to install new officers. (Courtesy Richards Studio D37649-1, Northwest Room at Tacoma Public Library.)

In 1914, Scuola Operaia and Missione Italiana was run by Napoleone Ghedini, who was paid by the Italian government to serve the Italian colony in Seattle. He taught Italian language classes, Sunday school, and Bible classes. Free medical visits for those unable to pay a doctor were available on Mondays. (Courtesy Frank Tesorieri.)

Four

THE ROLE OF THE CHURCH

From the mid-1850s to the late 1890s, Catholic missionaries ministered among the Indians, building beautiful churches, many that have been preserved to this day. The Jesuits were the first in the area, namely in Montana and Idaho and, later, called to Oregon and Washington. The two most important early Jesuits of Italian descent were Fr. Antonio Ravalli and Fr. Joseph Cataldo. While the old missions played a significant religious role among the tribes and early settlers, their nonreligious function was equally important.

From 1900 onwards, as the influx of immigrants in the Northwest grew, so too did the clergy's role. Priests assisted in protecting the rights of the vulnerable, especially the health and well-being of women and children; helping families navigate the laws and customs of their new nation; and strengthening their access to citizenship, labor markets, and sometimes capital. The church, through its many nonreligious groups, served as a social hub for newcomers, and Italians who might not have maintained regular attendance at Mass in Italy became devotees stateside.

In part due to language barriers and in part due to discrimination from Irish priests and their parishes, Italians in larger boroughs soon began raising money and volunteers to build their own churches. After the Second Vatican Council, Mass was celebrated much more frequently in Italian or even in a dialect. Italians asked their archbishop for Italian priests, many of whom became beloved by their flock precisely because they could understand one another better.

Some young Italian women heard a calling to serve as nuns. Throughout the Pacific Northwest, they taught school, ran orphanages, or worked as nurses in hospitals that they ran under the auspices of their diocese. Some, like Seattle native Virginia Cettolin, were called to the sisterhood because of the unbeknownst intercession of Frances Xavier Cabrini.

In just 35 years, Mother Cabrini, as she was known, established more than 60 institutions dedicated to caring for the sick, the uneducated, the abandoned, and the poor. When Virginia's mother, Erma, was extremely sick and lying in a Seattle hospital that Mother Cabrini founded, the whole family prayed to the saint for Erma's healing. Her mother's renewed health was a major impetus for Virginia to pursue a calling to serve as a teacher.

Mother Cabrini's group was the first-ever Italian female religious congregation to bear the title of missionary. In Seattle alone, she founded the Mount Carmel Mission on Beacon Hill, followed by the school at Our Lady of Mount Virgin, Sacred Heart Orphanage (now Villa Academy), and later, after many obstacles, Columbus Sanitarium (later renamed Cabrini Hospital) in 1916, one year before her death.

Some of the earliest Italians in the Pacific Northwest were Jesuit priests who served as missionaries among the native peoples. Fr. Joseph Cataldo from Sicily arrived on horseback in Spokane in 1866. He founded many missions in Montana and Washington—his most important being one named after him in Idaho. He bought land for a Jesuit college that became the renowned Gonzaga University in Spokane in 1881, which is extraordinary considering the city's population was only 1,500 by the time the college was completed in 1884. (Left, courtesy Eman Bonnici; below, courtesy Archives and Special Collections, Mansfield Library, University of Montana.)

According to historian Rev. Wilfred Schoenberg, Society of Jesus, many early Jesuits who came to the Northwest were from aristocratic Italian families. A multitalented Jesuit priest, Fr. Antonio Ravalli from Ferrara, would be among that upper class. He was an architect, builder, doctor, pharmacist, sculptor, and artist. A fabled figure, he traversed Montana on his Indian pony for 26 years to minister among the Salish people in their own language. A mission and a county are named in his honor. Fr. Anthony Ravalli served St. Mary's Mission in Montana from 1845 to 1850 and 1866 to 1884. Fr. Gregory Mengarini (not pictured) joined Fr. Pierre-Jean De Smet (not pictured), a Belgian priest and renowned peacemaker among the Indian tribes, in his journey from St. Louis to the Bitterroot Valley and helped establish St. Mary's Mission in the Rockies in 1841. Ravalli is pictured above and at left in a sculpture by Hank Wilkinson, from Monticello, Illinois. (Both, courtesy St. Mary's Mission, Montana.)

St. Michael the Archangel, on SW Fourth Avenue and Mill Street, has always been known as a national church for the Italians of Portland. In 1902, the majority of the brick building fund was raised in eight months, which is remarkable considering the average wage of uneducated immigrants was $30 a month and other churches were being built with wood. In 1910, Fr. Michael Balestra, the little man with the big heart, arrived, and he served his faithful *paesani* (countrymen) for over 40 years. His name became so synonymous with the church that it is engraved on an exterior lintel and the main hall is named after him. (Both, courtesy Archdiocese of Portland.)

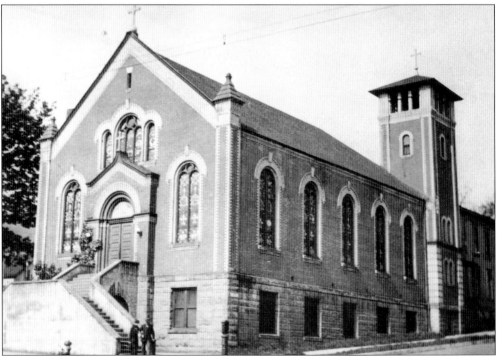

Our Lady of Mount Virgin, a national church, was built by Fr. Lodovico Caramello in 1915 on the foundation laid earlier by Blessed Mother Cabrini. Over its 100-years-plus history, scores of baptisms, first communions, confirmations, confessions, weddings, and funerals were held inside its hallowed walls. So, too, was it a community hub where newly landed immigrants sought information about room rentals, local jobs, and other Italians. In many families, three generations were Mount Virgin parishioners during Father Caramello's tenure. A colorful character, he endeared himself to his flock and non-Catholics alike. (Right, courtesy Chris Alfieri; below, courtesy Lisa Ursino.)

REV. LODOVICO CARAMELLO, S. J.
A. M. D. G.

In 1957, Ralph Alfieri wed Susan "Sue" Bradley at Our Lady of Mount Virgin Church. As a boy, Ralph stocked shelves for a nickel at his parents' deli. A lawyer by profession, he worked as an assistant attorney general and, later, in private practice in Seattle. (Courtesy Chris Alfieri.)

In 1911, Angela Rose Grandinetti (second row, far right) participated in her first holy communion ceremony at Our Lady of Mount Virgin in Seattle. (Courtesy Kathy Childers.)

This early-1920s photograph depicts Our Lady of Mount Virgin Parish School, built less than 10 years after the church held its first Italian Mass in Seattle. (Courtesy Lisa Ursino.)

Originally from San Marco la Catola, Italy, Fred Patricelli and Mary Riffaro met in Seattle and married in 1932 at Our Lady of Mount Virgin Church. (Courtesy Maia Santell.)

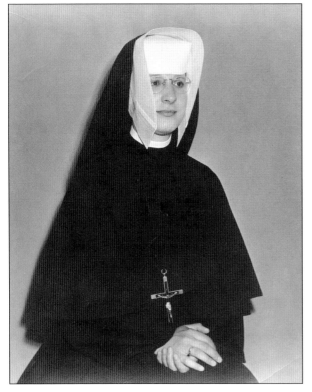

Theresa Fuda met Isaia Pighin at a dance in Seattle and married in 1930. They owned Quality Grocery, and Isaia also worked as a terrazzo and cement mason. (Courtesy Carrie Bergquist.)

Founder of the Sisters of the Sacred Heart and the first US citizen to be canonized a saint, Mother Frances Xavier Cabrini spent 13 years in Seattle. She helped found the Mount Carmel Mission, Villa Academy, and Columbus Hospital. She is commemorated in St. James Cathedral on First Hill, and when the church was rededicated in 1994, a few of her relics were sealed beneath the altar. (Courtesy Joe Salle.)

Here is Sister Mary Cabrini Cettolin, Ordinis Praedicatorum, (far left) with her fellow novices before their final profession to become nuns in 1960. Sister Cabrini was part of the Tacoma Dominicans, and she taught for 49 years at 11 different Catholic schools in Washington and California, including her first three years at Our Lady of Mount Virgin in Seattle. (Courtesy Virginia Cettolin.)

Founded in 1922, the Italian church in the Hilltop area of Tacoma was named after St. Rita of Cascia, a newly canonized saint in 1900, who intercedes on behalf of those needing help with improbable causes—something the Italian colony at the time could relate to. (Courtesy Francie Messina Jordan.)

An early mining town, Roslyn had a growing Catholic community in the late 1800s. It was central to ministering to its parishioners in 1892 during the worst coal mine disaster in Washington State's history. One Italian, Dominio Bianco, lost his life along with 44 others. It happened at the Northern Pacific Coal Company's No. 1 mine on Tuesday, May 10, at 1:45 p.m. Volatile methane gas built up in an airway that did not have enough ventilation in the lowest level of the mine, so even though the miners were in the process of connecting the airway to the level above, the gas detonated. (Courtesy author's collection.)

St. Philip Neri Church was built by Italians in 1912. In the 1940s, Paulist priest Fr. John Carvlin commissioned a school and convent. In 1950, a new church next door was designed by local architect Pietro Belluschi to accommodate a growing parish. (Courtesy Archdiocese of Portland.)

The Sisters of the Holy Child Jesus began teaching at the parish school in 1913. In 1928, the Sisters of the Holy Names of Jesus and Mary (pictured) took over, and they ran the school until 1973. (Courtesy Archdiocese of Portland.)

The Society of Our Lady of Pompeii was a charitable organization at St. Philip Neri that set out to help Italian immigrants get repatriated, although most of their work was in aid of children, whether they were sick or had lost their families. (Courtesy Archdiocese of Portland.)

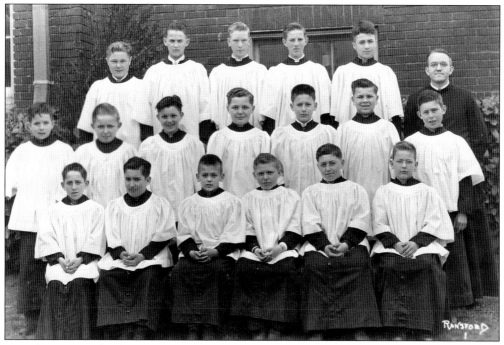

In 1950 at Our Lady of Mount Virgin, it was not a difficult task for the priest to recruit altar boys. Altar boys attend to the supporting tasks at the altar while the priest celebrates Mass. (Courtesy Chris Alfieri.)

St. Michael's Mission Church in the Hillyard neighborhood of Spokane was the main place of worship for Catholic Italians in the early years of their immigrant adventure. Constructed in the mid-1800s and later led by Fr. Joseph Cataldo, it served as the first Catholic mission east of the Mississippi and then as a Jesuit seminary on land on which Gonzaga University now sits. (Courtesy Historic American Buildings Survey, National Park Service.)

Five

AT WAR

It was not enough that Italy gave up over 5 million soldiers to serve in World War I, much less losing over 650,000 of them in battle. But at the outbreak of World War II, Italy was again a war zone and demanding territory it thought it deserved 20 years earlier and did not get. When Italy switched to the Allied side in 1943, the government cut a deal with the Americans. Any captured Italian soldier would be brought stateside to shore up the domestic labor shortage and military efforts. Almost 15,000 Italian soldiers, known as Italian Service Units, lived and worked in minor-security camps throughout the United States.

The Italian soldiers wore a variation of an American uniform but with an "Italy" patch sewn on their left sleeve. Stationed around the Northwest, they were an anomaly as service and support troops. These men, caught in the middle, found themselves far from home, unsure of who their friends and enemies were. Americans were also not sure what to make of them—some were wary of a defeated army in their midst, while others were welcoming to their fellow countrymen.

Most commissioned officers were allowed generous leave and were checked out of the camps by local families on weekend and festival days. They broke bread with them, attended Mass, played games, frequented dances, drank wine, and ate familiar meals, but then they returned to the camp by nightfall to satisfy curfew requirements. They became one of the family, and some even married into their host families.

During the war, the majority of Italian citizens aged 14 and over living in the United States were considered enemy aliens. Based on their registrations, there were approximately 700,000 in 1939. Many were investigated, and some were arrested and detained. Italians who lived in America but had not yet become citizens found themselves in a precarious place—the men most especially. Some were rounded up like the Japanese and Germans and put in camps, though separate from the Italian soldiers. Countless people lost their jobs, were forced to speak only English in public, and endured endless taunting, or worse, destruction or forfeiture of property. Possessions were seized, including radios, or at the least, they had their short-wave capability disabled.

Families rushed to get naturalization papers, and many men signed up to serve, which guaranteed them automatic citizenship. America was their home, and they wanted to do their duty, even if it meant fighting the citizenry of their ancestral homeland. Italian American women who were born in the United States or had become naturalized and either married prisoners of wars or Italians without American citizenship lost theirs, which many eventually regained but not for many years later.

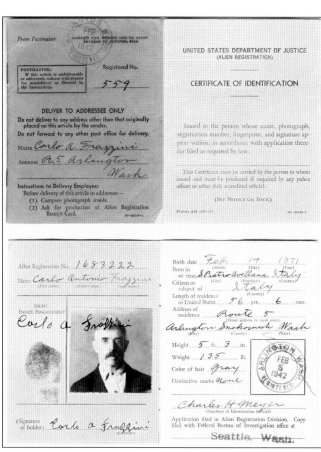

During World War II, German, Italian, and Japanese citizens and aliens were required to register with the US Department of Justice. They had to carry this alien identification with them at all times and produce it if asked by any police or other official. (Left, courtesy Gene Frazzini; below, courtesy Marilyn Gatto.)

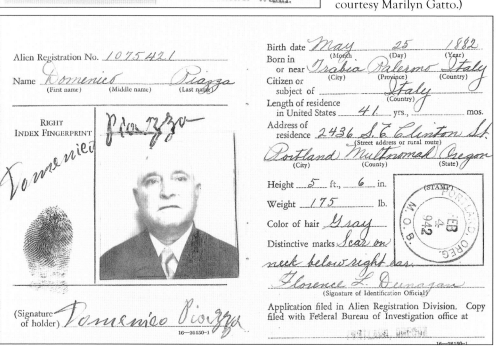

In contrast to alien registration in World War II, the Portland mayor honored World War I US soldiers of Italian descent at a dinner held near Fort Vancouver in 1918. Twenty-five years later, Italian citizens were held in a prisoner of war camp at the same location. (Courtesy City of Portland Archives.)

M. G. MONTREZZA
LAWYER
SUITE 222-4 HENRY BLDG.

PORTLAND, OREGON. March 6, 1918.

SUBJECT:

Mayor Geo. L. Baker,
City Hall,
Portland, Ore.

Dear Sir:-

The Italian Colony of Portland on Saturday evening, March 9, will entertain some seventy U. S. Soldiers of Italian extraction now at Vancouver, Wash., by giving in their honor a banquet and dance at the Woodmen of the World's Hall, East 6th and East Alder Streets, this City, and I am requested by the Committee in charge of the affair to extend to you a cordial invitation to attend and deliver an address to the boys.

The Italians of our City would immensely appreciate your presence on that date and kindly notify the writer, whether or not it shall be convenient and possible for you to gratify their wish.

A delegation of the Committee shall await upon you at the W. of the W. Hall's door at 7:30 P.M.

With kindest personal regards, I am, dear sir,

Your truly,

M. G. Montrezza

OFFICE OF GOVERNOR

A STATEMENT BY THE GOVERNOR:

I wish to call to the attention of all Japanese, Germans and Italians residing in Washington who are not citizens of the United States that the federal Department of Justice has ordered that they obtain certificates of identification.

The applications for certificates of registration will be accepted at first or second class or county seat post offices from Monday, February 2, 1942, through Saturday, February 7. Aliens less than 14 years of age are exempt under the order issued by the Department of Justice.

The applicants must carry with them their alien registration receipt card and three unmounted photographs of themselves, with light background, 2 inches by 2 inches in size. The photographs must have been taken within 30 days previous to the application, from a front view, and without a hat. The applicant may be accompanied by a friend or relative and may be assisted if the applicant is unable to write. There will be no expense.

As the State of Washington has considerable numbers of non-citizen German, Japanese and Italian residents it is essential that there be strict compliance with the Department of Justice's order.

In 1942, Gov. Arthur Langlie of Washington issued a statement reminding that, according to an edict of the Department of Justice, all Germans, Japanese, and Italians who were not US citizens must register as aliens. (Courtesy White River Valley Museum.)

THE KLAN RIDES AGAIN

From: KU KLUX KLAN, Inc. P.O. Box 527, Seattle, Wash.

To: HONORABLE MEMBERS OF THE CITY COUNCIL, Seattle, Wash.

Subject: INVESTIGATION. November 16th, 1937.

The KU KLUX KLAN notes that one Howard G. Costigan, as quoted by the P.-I. of last Sunday, November 14th, 1937, asks an investigation of the KU KLUX KLAN in Seattle.

We note also that 2 of your Members, as quoted, as asking investigation of the Silver Shirts - the Nazi movement, along with the Klan.

May we ask why the Italian Fascists also in Seattle, are not included?

Is there any thing more deadly - more sinister - to American Democracy, than Fascism, Naziism and Communism. The KU KLUX KLAN classes all these as un-American, with Communism as the most dangerous of the three.

The KU KLUX KLAN are ALL AMERICANS, no ism- no symbol - no salute - no flag - except to salute the Stars and Stripes, and the Stars and Stripes is OUR ONLY FLAG.

We invite investigation by your Body, to the fullest extent.

Yours for AMERICA FOR AMERICANS,

cc- Editors of   KU KLUX KLAN, Inc., By order of Chief of Staff,
Seattle Times;
Seattle Post-Intelligencer;   *John Reed*
Seattle Star.
                         John Reed, Address P.O. Box 527, Seattle, Wash.

COMMUNISM WILL NOT BE TOLERATED

Many may not realize that the Ku Klux Klan had a presence in the Pacific Northwest, and this letter proves it. The note was sent on Klan letterhead to the Seattle City Council, which wanted both the Klan and the Silver Shirts (Nazi sympathizers) investigated. The Klan wanted to know why the Italian fascists were not being questioned the same as the others. (Courtesy Seattle Municipal Archives.)

The father of nuclear science in America, Enrico Fermi came to America to teach and, later, spent time in Hanford, Washington, developing the atomic bomb during World War II. In 1944, he inserted the first uranium slug into the "B" pile nuclear reactor. (Courtesy Atomic Heritage Foundation.)

During World War I and World War II, foreign-born soldiers were 18 and 3 percent, respectively, of the US armed forces, many of them Italians. Men like Umberto Barei and Joe Salle, shown at right around 1918 and below around 1942, respectively, in their US Army uniforms, volunteered to serve to prove their loyalty to their adopted homeland. Some soldiers signed up without knowing much English, and the military instituted language and civics classes to help immigrants seamlessly integrate into American culture and society. Congress even passed legislation to allow expedited naturalization of these noncitizens. Thousands of immigrants lost their lives in service of this country, often before obtaining their American citizenship. (Right, courtesy No. 2018.033.001, Renton History Museum; below, courtesy Joe Salle.)

Cousins Albert Colaianni (left) and Rico Benedetti (right) from Pocatello, Idaho, served in World War II—Albert was in the Army Air Corps, and Rico was with the 776th Tank Destroyer Battalion. (Courtesy Rayna Valentine.)

NOT MARRIED
BUT WILLING TO BE

After the attack on Pearl Harbor, Ricardo Cettolin left high school to join the US Navy. He served in the Navy as a gunner's mate second class on merchant ships in the Atlantic during World War II. He received an American Arms Medal, European/African Arms Medal, a Good Conduct Medal, and a World War II Victory Medal for his service. (Courtesy Virginia Cettolin.)

The 1907 Expatriation Act, which linked a woman's US citizenship to that of their husband's citizenship after marriage, meant that many women in the Pacific Northwest lost their citizenship because they either married Italian prisoners of war or men from the Italian Service Units, a division of the US armed forces. Post marriage, these women were required to place "alien" on US Census forms. This is what happened to the Delaurenti sisters. From left to right, Mary Delaurenti with her son Pete and Theresa Delaurenti Giuliani with her daughter Grace are pictured in 1921 in Newcastle, Washington. In reverse, American men who married Italian women were lauded rather than treated as suspicious. In 1922, the Cable Act was passed, thanks to the suffragettes, ending the practice of stripping citizenship from American-born women who married foreign-born men. (Courtesy No. 2015.011.071, Renton History Museum.)

Several Italian Americans served as Army Air Corps pilots stationed in Gearhart, Oregon, during

World War II. (Courtesy US Army Signal Corps, Fort Vancouver.)

On the night of August 14, 1944, at the Fort Lawton military base in Seattle, the segregated African American soldiers had a tense exchange with some Italian prisoners of war that led to a riot. Interracial tensions had been building for weeks because the black troops believed Italian prisoners were receiving better treatment and facilities. The Italians also enjoyed freedoms and privileges outside the camp that excluded black troops. Guglielmo Olivotto was lynched during the riot, prompting a shoddy investigation that resulted in the largest court martial of World War II and the conviction of 23 black soldiers with sentences ranging from 1 to 15 years. The judgement shocked the nation; however, years later, many received pardons. Olivotto's grave bears a broken Roman column, a marker of a life cut short. (Courtesy author's collection.)

For both the Axis and Allied powers, war caused shortages. The one felt by everyone was food. Fuel and transport trucks were requisitioned for the war effort, so shipping fresh food was limited and Victory Gardens were encouraged. Ration books helped ensure equitable distribution among Americans. (Courtesy Mercedes Loprinzi.)

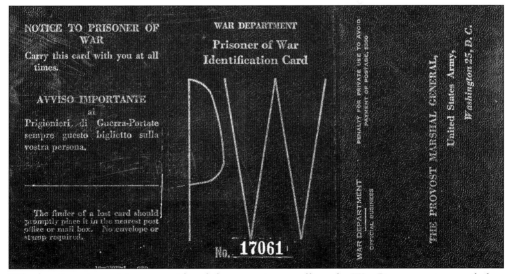

Whether American citizens considered them captives or allies, the War Department nevertheless issued POW identification cards in English with Italian translation to over 50,000 Italians captured in North Africa in World War II. (Courtesy Oregon Historical Society.)

During the 1940s, the Blister Rust Camp in Kalispell Bay, Idaho, held a few hundred Italian prisoners of war. Prisoners of war had to build and maintain their lodgings and cook for themselves, and yet despite being internees, they still managed to be well-suited and booted. (Both, courtesy Priest Lake Museum.)

Italian Internee Program-Kalispell Bay '43

Members of Italian Service Units stationed in Fort Vancouver used their spare time to whittle wood, craft utilitarian objects like wooden serving trays, or custom engrave their cigarette lighters. (Photographs by US Army Signal Corps, Fort Vancouver, courtesy Oregon Historical Society.)

Italian prisoners of war who were officers were often checked out of their camp by local families for a day over the weekend. These prisoners of war were considered one of the family and sometimes even became an official member. (Courtesy Rainier Valley Historical Society.)

John Ursino from Seattle was honorably discharged from the Marines in 1946 in San Diego. He served with distinction as part of special weapons battalions and anti-aircraft divisions in Guadalcanal, Iwo Jima, and the Battle of Tarawa. (Courtesy Lisa Ursino.)

Six

AT WORK

It was the love of providing for their families better than they could in Italy that drove millions to leave their beloved towns and immigrate to America. These laborers wanted familiar foods and produce—like garlic, eggplant, artichokes, and broccoli—which were not plentiful or known then. They bought from Italian merchants who set up shop as produce sellers, grocers, butchers, bakers, and pasta makers. In the early years, only about 20 percent of men in the Italian colonies were engaged in business and professional pursuits such as druggists, doctors, dentists, tailors, lawyers, and real estate agents.

Unskilled men worked hard labor jobs like tie hacking for the Northern Pacific Railroad in Priest River, Idaho; millwork for Bethlehem Steel; forging iron for Isaacson Ironworks; mining clay for paving brick in Taylor and coal in Franklin; running (and later owning) garbage-collecting crews and constructing water mains, sewer lines, highways, and bridges in Seattle, Tacoma, Spokane, and Portland; and logging in Hoquiam and North Bend for lumber, window sashes, and roof tiles. Several Italian families raised dairy cattle like the Gualtieris on Magnolia Bluff (later Bothell), the Grecos in Roslyn, and the Riccis, Spadas, Caveleros, Segales, and Rossellis in Snohomish County. Many Italian names appear on historic maps that include rivers, lakes, parks, and homesteads, and one family, the Sartoris of Renton, even offered land for such public service projects as a cemetery, a Carnegie library, and a school.

Most women pioneers did not work outside the home, though some did. A few ran boardinghouses, became nurses and teachers, or helped their husbands in the family grocery, restaurant, or homestead. In one case, Mary Stella Marinocci of Tacoma raised silkworms. She tried her hand at it for a few years like she had in the old country, but it was a lot of work to find mulberry tree leaves to feed the voracious eaters. Even though it was next to impossible to get silk from Japan for manufacturing stockings once the war started, her business died because it was not economically feasible. Many women called into wartime service still found time to volunteer through social clubs, churches, and as Red Cross nurse's aides—all while caring for their children, keeping their house, growing produce, and balancing the family's budget.

Despite being called out for being ignorant and illiterate, Italians kept at their work, helped one another, and got on with life with the love and determination of their families. In whatever someone endeavors to take on as their life's work or passion, a family's support is everything—and that is certainly the case for Italian Americans.

ITALIANS NOT WANTED.

Iowa caal operators should think twice before they begin the importation of Italians and other such people to work their mines. After they have thought twice they should decide not to take such steps. Italian miners are not wanted. They are not congenial to Iowa. Our people can make no place for them in the commonwealth. They are not in sympathy with our institutions. They are not desirable elements in the population. With others of similar character they have cursed Pennsylvania, Ohio, Nevada and other states. The cheapness of their labor is not economy. It is extravagance of the worst kind. They will not educate. They have poor conception of our standard of morality. They are not self-governing. Wherever they are to be found in considerable numbers that locality bears every evidence of blight.

Note the two newspaper articles, published 15 years apart, from the Pacific Northwest and Iowa. Compare the sentiment in the 1895 Pacific Northwest clipping below, where Italians have "sterling qualities" and are "industrious," "peaceful," and "thrifty" to the 1910 Iowa one at left, where they are defined as "not congenial," "not in sympathy with our institutions," "not desirable," have "a poor conception of morality," and so on. The sympathies of Americans for some immigrants in favor of others have always waxed and waned like the moon and varied from one part of the country to the other. Throughout history, disparaging comments have been made about a people without thought or enough understanding; in this case, and even now, ethnic groups are put into a class not of their own making and, often, without recourse to prove themselves otherwise. (Left, courtesy *Catholic Northwest Progress*; below, courtesy *Gazzetta Italiana*.)

ITALIANS AS CITIZENS.

The editor of the New York World pays a well deserved tribute to the Italian contingent in the United States. The editorial "Why are Italians classed as undesirable citizens?" In response the editor of the World says:

"Usually it is safe to say such classification is made by unthinking persons unacquainted with the sterling qualities of the great mass of Italian immigrants. In the vast numbers which reach these shores from Italy there are undoubtedly many whom the mother country is glad to lose, but this class makes up but a very small proportion of the whole. Generally the Italian immigrant is industrious, peaceful and thrifty, courteously considerate of the rights of others and eager to improve the conditions of himself and his family. The success of these Italians and the places they are winning in industrial and commercial America constitute the best defense against the slanders of which our correspondent writes."

Published Every Friday since 1910

GAZZETTA ITALIANA
AN AMERICAN NEWSPAPER
Owned, Edited and Printed by American Citizens
for American Readers of Italian Extraction

Publisher and Editor ....F. M. Bassetti

1801 Rainier Avenue   Seattle 44, Wash.   PR. 7177

Subscription Rate   U. S., $2.00 per year; Foreign, $3.00

Entered as Second Class Matter, April 21, 1928, at the Post
Office at Seattle, Wash., under Act of March 3, 1879

Besides barbershops, corner grocery stores, churches, and bulletins from local clubs, newspapers were the main organs for news for early immigrants. Portland had the *Tribuna* and Spokane had the *Columbus Record*. In Seattle, newspaper editors, like Federico "Fred" Bassetti (*Gazzetta Italiana*) and Nicola Paolella (*Washington Courier*, which later became *Gazzetta Italiana*), were instrumental in publishing the earliest Italian-language newspapers in the Pacific Northwest. Nicola, who served for a time as the Italian consul in Seattle, also hosted a radio show in the city for over 25 years. These services garnered him a knighthood by the Italian government. (Both, courtesy *Gazzetta Italiana*, Special Collections, University of Washington.)

He Was First President

NICOLA PAOLELLA

Nicola Paolella was the first president of the Italian Club. His term was for the year of 1920 He also served as president in 1924. Nicola was one of the founders of the Italian Club. He had a long and illustrious career in our community He came to America a well-educated pharmacist and practised in Seattle for many years. He was well known for his knowledge of Italian Culture. During his many years he was the Italian Consul and presented the Italian Hour on radio as recently as in the 1950s. In his latter years he came to be fondly known as the "Dean of the Italian Colony."

On April 29, 1899, a violent explosion set by about 1,000 enraged striking miners destroyed the Bunker Hill and Sullivan Mill in Wardner, Idaho, with over 4,000 pounds of dynamite. The smoking rubble was the result of a drawn-out labor dispute between union supporters, including many Italians, and the mine's owners. (Courtesy University of Idaho Library.)

Discoveries of gold, silver, lead, and copper veins in the Craters of the Moon region led to years of extracting, processing, and transporting minerals, which greatly influenced Idaho's development as a state. Here is an 1887 pay sheet for one mining concern that lists employees, occupations, amount borrowed from the company store, and so on. At the top of the list is an Italian, O. Sarno. (Courtesy Idaho Historical Society.)

Besides building railroads in Idaho, men worked on repairing refrigerated railcars for the Pacific Fruit Express (PFE). A partnership between the Southern Pacific and Union Pacific railroads, PFE was created so that perishable fruits from the West could be grown year-round and shipped all over the country without spoilage. Railcars were also for shipping lumber, and Italian men could be found felling trees and cutting railroad ties for railroad construction. In the Boise National Forest in April 1912, Italian "station men," as they were known, crossed this footbridge to begin grading and burning brush when the footbridge gave way and drowned two of them. (Above, courtesy Idaho State Historical Society; below, courtesy Idaho State Archives.)

In the late 19th century, immigrant loggers in Grays Harbor, Washington, used ox teams to drag logs to the Satsop Railroad in Big Skookum. On rare days off and yearning for a taste of home, these loggers saved up and headed to Aberdeen. At the Toscano Café, owned by Guido Rosi, they enjoyed—with gusto—a hard-earned Italian dinner. (Courtesy Great Eastern Photographic and Advertising Company.)

In the early 1900s, on the lower Columbia River, close to the once-mighty river's mouth, a fleet of butterflies flitted about. At least that was what the triangular sails set perpendicular to one another made these gillnet fishing boats look like. Helmed mostly by Scandinavians, though Italians gave it a go, too, they fished for salmon and tuna, which were sold to the canneries in Astoria. (Courtesy Tom McCurry.)

Rich with coal deposits, Western Washington was a boon for early Italians and Welsh who found employment in the state's largest mines in Roslyn, Black Diamond, Renton, Newcastle, Centralia, and Bellingham. Ore lore is tied tightly to railway construction, which helped Western expansion, thanks to the hard labor of Italians in both these industries. When the Black Diamond Coal Mining company discovered a seam of coal near the Green River in early 1880, it built Mine No. 11, which was at one time the largest coal mine in Western Washington. To transport men, supplies, and coal, a Columbia & Puget Sound rail line ran from Renton to Black Diamond. (Right, courtesy Washington Division of Mines; below, courtesy Black Diamond History Museum.)

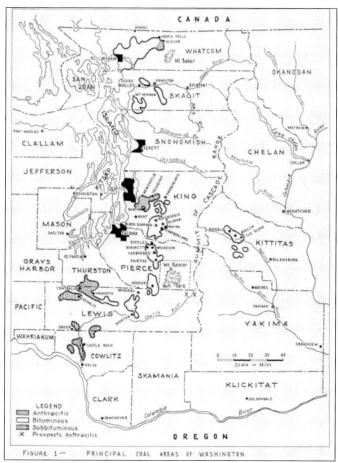

FIGURE 1 — PRINCIPAL COAL AREAS OF WASHINGTON

71

By the end of the 1930s, Pacific Coast Coal Company, one of the many companies that operated the company town of Black Diamond, closed up its mines due to low demand for coal. From the 1880s until then, immigrants from Italy and Wales worked 10- to 12-hour days for $1.50 a day. By World War I, they had a union with an $8 a day pay rate. It was dangerous work for little pay, and mine disasters took many a life. Franklin was a nearby company town where there was housing, a store, a church, and other facilities. Immigrants formed enclaves based on their countries of origin. "Dago Town" was the name for the Italian one among "Swede Town," "Welsh Town," and so on. The various groups often came together for ethnic potlucks and shared food and a bit of culture with one another. (Both, courtesy Black Diamond History Museum.)

Brothers Dario and John Bulgarelli worked at the Denny Clay and Coal Company in Taylor, and by 1910, it was one of the most important businesses in the Renton, Washington, area. The company opened on the banks of the Cedar River and began producing clay and terra-cotta bricks, firmly establishing the town as the "Paving Brick Capital of the World." Renton, unlike other towns, used its coal for manufacturing. (Courtesy Carrie Bergquist.)

Besides working in deep mine shafts, Italian crews paved roads around Black Diamond. (Courtesy Black Diamond History Museum.)

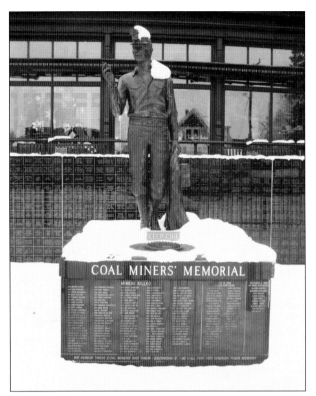

In May 1892, the townspeople of Roslyn lined their main street for a funeral procession for victims of a horrific explosion that shut down the No. 1 Mine. Forty-five men, one of them Italian, died when a buildup of methane gas exploded—just another example of how dangerous coal mining can be. That Italian miner along with other immigrants are memorialized in the town center (left) and in the Italian section of the Roslyn Cemetery (below). (Both, courtesy author's collection.)

After major labor strikes in 1886 and 1890 across New York, a proposal was put forth for a celebration to be held in September that would include a street parade and picnic, which "would publicly show the strength and esprit de corps of the trade and labor organizations," according to the proposal. This photograph is of Seattle's 1909 Labor Day celebration. (Courtesy Washington State Archives.)

In Portland, Dr. Marie Equi, likely the first Italian woman physician in Oregon, fought for labor rights and women's suffrage, even paying for it with time in jail. After volunteering during the 1906 San Francisco Earthquake as a US Army doctor, she was commended by President Roosevelt for her relief work. Back in her Portland practice, she treated primarily working-class women and children, often at no charge, until 1930. (Courtesy Oregon Historical Society.)

Unlike pioneering Dr. Equi, most
Italian women of her time were not
professionals, but equally important,
they stayed home and cared for their
families. The war years were especially
challenging, and women made the most
of what they had. Household chores like
washing, cleaning, and cooking occupied
much of their day. (Left, courtesy
Housing Authority of Portland; below,
courtesy Seattle Municipal Archives.)

Lucia DeSanza was quite talented and was able to do quite well for herself working at home in Idaho. She is pictured with daughters Olga (left) and Emilia (right) about 1915, and all are wearing Lucia's creations. Unfortunately, Olga died in 1933 at 24 years old of meningitis on the eve of her wedding, and her sister Emilia died at 13 years old of the flu. Some Italian women helped in their families' businesses or found work as secretaries, retail clerks, or telephone operators as those jobs became available. Emilia Russo (right) worked a switchboard in Seattle, but she often acted as a translator, too, because immigrants, whose first language was not English, needed help. (Right, courtesy Joe Salle; below, courtesy Rayna Valentine.)

As Italian colonies became more established and prosperous around the Pacific Northwest, Italians sought to gather regularly and built meeting halls suited for their purposes, like the Italian Federation Building in Portland. Many Italians belonged to several social groups and often shared premises for events and celebrations. Some social groups had offices, pool halls, and dining facilities. (Courtesy Public Works Administration.)

Vegetable peddlers were prolific in the Pacific Northwest. Most Italians had gardens in Italy and grew their own produce to feed their families, and some made a business out of it in America. In the 1920s, John Aragone's garden in Spokane employed many farmworkers. (Courtesy Northwest Museum.)

Charles Loprinzi, a produce seller, grew a lot of spinach and claimed the humble vegetable as the reason his "strongmen" sons could lift so much iron. The family grew up as vegetarians and loved the spaghetti their father fed them. (Courtesy Mercedes Loprinzi.)

Portland truck farmer Calogero "Sam" Amato prospered in the produce business. (Courtesy Amato family.)

Nunzio "Nick" Marzano's family immigrated to Chicago from Ricigliano, a small town in Campania, Italy. The family had a cousin in Tacoma who offered to help Nick find work, so he headed west. Before World War II, he sold produce door-to-door. In the 1950s, he opened a fruit stand on South Tacoma Way that was prosperous for many years. (Courtesy Joe Munizza.)

The Italian Delicatessen & Grocery Co. was doing well in 1915, and the owner and his employees proudly posed for this photograph with their new truck. From left to right are John Quilici (owner), an unidentified man with a barrel, Lorenzo Giusti, "Rosino" Martini, Italo Montecarlo, and Battista Giannini. (Courtesy Al C. Giusti.)

In the foothills of the Blue Mountains, early immigrants, from both Northern and Southern Italy, started farming onions. What they planted would become known as Walla Walla sweet onions. Single men with the surnames Orsini (1857), Saturno-Breen (1876), Arbini (1890), Locati (1905), and Castoldi (1926)—to name a few—arrived first to the area, and later, they brought their families over or started them here. It was not long before Italians and onions became synonymous with the Eastern Washington town of Walla Walla. That varietal was eventually designated the state vegetable—all thanks to a Frenchman from Corsica named Pete Pieri. That humble vegetable provided all kinds of sustenance to those early Italian pioneers and their descendants today. One place those onions were sold was the Pike Place Market in Seattle. (Above, courtesy Whitman College and Northwest Archives; below, courtesy Seattle Municipal Archives.)

In 1946, Pete's Italian Grocery, in the lower level of Seattle's famous Pike Place Market, started small but did not stay there. Over the years, Pete and Mae DeLaurenti introduced Seattle to imported meats, cheeses, and dry goods. When they retired in 1972 and their son Louie bought the business, now DeLaurenti Food & Wine, he moved it to street level, where it has been ever since. (Above, courtesy Seattle Municipal Archives; below, courtesy author's collection.)

Brothers and vegetable sellers Pat and Nick Vacca farmed on a hillside above Sick's Stadium in Seattle. In the 1930s and 1940s, the brothers had a clear view of the games as they tended their garden. It was not long before friends, neighbors, and Seattleites galore saw the benefit of watching ball games from the Vaccas' garden without having to pay admission, hence the hillside's nickname, "Tightwad Hill." (Above, courtesy Museum of History and Industry; below, courtesy Chris Alfieri.)

Corno's Food Market was located at 711 SE Martin Luther King Jr. Boulevard (formerly Santa Barbara Avenue). Established by Jimmy Corno and his family in the early 1950s, it was one of several Italian produce sellers that made up "Produce Row" in Portland. Burt Reynolds filmed a famous scene on the grocer's roof for his 1989 movie *Breaking In*. The city razed the building in 2006–2007. (Above, courtesy Jan Schoen; below, courtesy Portland Municipal Archives.)

In Portland's early years, dozens of wholesale producers like Rinella Produce, Corno's Produce, and Sheridan Fruit Company formed Produce Row. Pioneer Fruit Distributors began in 1907 when Salvatore Dindia, with a horse and wagon, peddled his produce around the city alongside about 100 similar rigs and their owners. In the 1970s, the company was the oldest wholesale produce house in Portland continuously owned by the same family. (Above, courtesy Dindia family; below, courtesy Portland Municipal Archives.)

Portland Archives, A2009-009.2435.

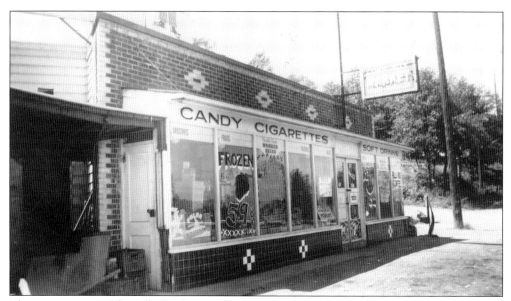

Three generations of the Salle family owned and operated a community market and butcher shop in various Seattle locations for over 100 years. "Home of the Live Butcher" was a moniker that made them well known throughout the region until they closed up shop in 2011. (Courtesy Joe Salle.)

Wholesale food importer and later well-known retailer "Big John" Croce, owner of Pacific Food Importers, loved food, family, and fun. He founded the annual Festa Italiana and the annual homemade wine tasting event, which reached its 50th year in 2023. A generous soul with a big smile, John was a pillar of the Italian community in Seattle. (Courtesy Sylvia Croce.)

In the early 1900s, Italians faced discrimination and were ridiculed because Americans could not pronounce their names. Many Italian businesses repurposed names that would not pose problems, which is how, though unrelated, the French Bakery in Seattle and Portland got their name. In 1917, the Seattle French Bakery was owned by Philip Sugia, and later several partners, until Sugia sold his interest in 1925. It had several owners until it was purchased by Gai's Bakery. The Chiotti family started the French Bakery in Portland in 1903. It evolved into Pierre's French Bakery in 1970. In 1992, it merged with Gai's Bakery, founded by Giglio Gai, who started baking some French bread of his own in 1931. (Courtesy Maia Santell and Dean Chiotti.)

Santo "Sam" and Sophie Porco married in 1932 and, soon after, opened S.P. Bakery. It became THE bakery in town, with all the bigwigs making it their favorite bakery for cakes for all their special occasions. Sam's generosity was boundless. He kept cookie samples for customers' children and volunteered for 30 years with the Portland Police Sunshine Division, delivering food baskets to the needy. (Both, courtesy Barbara Porco.)

Remo Borracchini's father started the family bakery in his Garlic Gulch basement in 1922, supplying many of the Italian families and groceries in the neighborhood with bread. In 1935, at the age of five, Remo began working in the bakery, eventually taking over the business in the 1950s. Up until a fire consumed the building on May 29, 2022, Borracchini's was known as one of the best Italian bakeries in Seattle. (Courtesy Rainier Valley Historical Society.)

Together with his mom, Dorothy, Art Oberto, Seattle's "Sausage and Jerky King," took over the sausage company at 16 when his father, Constantino, died suddenly in 1943. The company's Italian flag-inspired logo graced everything from paper hats their factory workers wore to the Jerky Mobile, a 1950s Lincoln that Art drove around town, and to the legendary hydroplanes they sponsored at the city's annual Seafair. (Courtesy San Gennaro Festival.)

In 1957, Alfieri's Fine Foods served over 300 pizzas a day. The founder, Raffaello "Ralph" Alfieri, immigrated in 1920 from Morrone del Sannio, Campobasso, when he was 12. He was a pioneer in convenience specialty foods manufacture and sales. Its ravioli and cannelloni were served at the Seattle Space Needle restaurant for decades. The ravioli, spaghetti sauce, and pizzas were sold to Reser's Foods, Safeway, the Four Seasons Hotel, bakeries like Borracchini's and Gai's, and Oberto Sausage. Alfieri designed two machines that were manufactured in Italy: one that rolled pizza dough to his desired thickness and a ravioli one to keep up with demand. Before this, the Alfieri family owned and operated a grocery store starting in 1932 in the heart of Garlic Gulch and ran it until 1956, when big chain groceries made competition difficult. (Both, courtesy Chris Alfieri.)

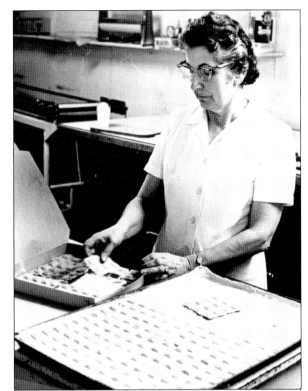

Angelina "Grandma" Marra Alfieri prepares a ravioli order for a customer. Cranking out small pizzas, the production line includes, from the foreground to the rear, Mary Perry, Ange Alfieri, Arlene Perry (Sam and Mary's daughter), Sam Perry, and Ralph Alfieri. For a while, Sam opened his own Sam's Meats location. (Both, courtesy Chris Alfieri.)

G. Arata & Sons operated a successful wholesale liquor distribution business before Prohibition took its toll. For some, Prohibition and the Depression offered challenges, but if one were a savvy entrepreneur like Philip Sugia, he or she might see opportunities where others saw lawlessness. When the Grand Coulee Dam was under construction, Philip not only managed a brothel, but by coestablishing the National Wine Company (NAWICO), he partook in Prohibition-era bootlegging, too. (Above, courtesy Oregon Historical Society; below, courtesy Maia Santell.)

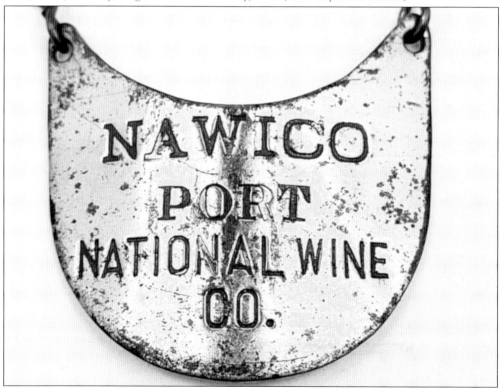

Victor Rosellini operated several fine dining restaurants that were popular for many years in the Seattle area. (Courtesy author's collection.)

OUR PLEASURE
. . . to serve you
Royally!

Rosellini's Restaurants of Renown

VICTOR'S 610 PINE	Rosellini's FOUR-10
featuring Florentine delicacies from the celebrated cucina of John Poggetti	chosen by Holiday Magazine as tops in dining distinction, superb service
■	■
Melodic diversion nightly in the 610 cocktail lounge	Best of cocktail circuit acts nightly in the Boulevard Room
■	■
610 PINE ST. MA 4-2355	410 UNIV. PLAZA MA 4-5464

A red-and-white checkerboard tablecloth kind of a place, Gasperetti's Roma Café was operated by brothers William and John Gasperetti, who were sons of Italian immigrants from Florence. For almost 40 years, the restaurant was popular and patronized by famous athletes, local and well-known politicians, and a host of regulars. (Courtesy Bob Gasperetti.)

Like many Italians back in Italy, Ciro Pasciuto had a passion for cooking and baking that he brought to his adopted homeland. In 1989, he turned his hobby of baking Italian-style bread into a favorite of Seattle-area restaurants and hotels. Later, Americans coast-to-coast fell in love with the family's award-winning Croccantini® ("crunchy little bites") crackers, reminiscent of rustic flatbread from home. (Courtesy Kim Pasciuto and La Panzanella Artisanal Foods Co.)

Antonio Magnano landed in Seattle in the late 1890s, and in 1903, he founded A. Magnano & Sons, which is famous for its Napoleon Olive Oil. Now known as the Napoleon Company, the fourth generation of Magnanos has grown its selection of dry goods beyond olive oil and expanded the business into several states. (Courtesy Tony Magnano.)

When starting a business, it is often said, "Do what you know." For Italians, that is food and wine, both making and selling it. Pagni & Lenti (later Pagni & Sons Grocery, not shown) and Eagle Macaroni Manufacturing were two early Tacoma stalwarts until Pagni's closed in 1940—nine years after Pietro Pagni's death—and a massive fire forced the Eagle factory to close in 1915. (Courtesy Washington State Historical Society.)

Guido Cinelli immigrated from Italy to Tacoma in 1902 and started manufacturing macaroni and importing Italian foods for his G. Cinelli Company. Interestingly, in 1923, the company was listed in the federal Annual Report of Patents for its "Washington Brand Italian Virgin Olive Oil" and advertised it as "food with medicinal virtue." (Courtesy Northwest Room at Tacoma Public Library.)

For 40 years, legendary brothers Angelo, Barney, and John Carnino operated a garage and built and raced cars at No-Bar, Sea-Tac, and Aurora racetracks. (Courtesy Black Diamond History Museum.)

One of the first fire commissioners for the town of Black Diamond was an Italian, as were two of the volunteers, Jules Dal Santo and Don Malgarini (not pictured). From left to right are commissioner John B. Lombardini Jr., commissioner W. Frank Horne, commissioner Evan S. Thomas, and fire chief Thomas Zumek of King County Fire Protection District No. 17. (Courtesy Black Diamond Historical Society.)

A real artisan in metal, Saveri Russo worked at the famous Washington Ironworks, where the modern logging engine was perfected and is the recognized standard worldwide. (Courtesy Joe Salle.)

Construction, another one of the heavy-labor industries that immigrants found themselves in, was especially important for Italians. Family-owned and -operated for decades, Fiorito Brothers, Northwest Construction, Thomas Scalzo, Scarsella, and others are well known in Seattle. (Courtesy Chris Alfieri.)

Portland Archives, A2004-002.4824

Pietro Belluschi became dean of the Massachusetts Institute of Technology's School of Architecture after successfully managing his own firm in Portland (1942–1950). Fred Bassetti, too, had several Seattle firms (1950–1991). As visionaries and craftsmen, both men shared a passion for Northwest Modernism and contributed significantly to their profession. (Left, courtesy City of Portland Archives; below, courtesy Bassetti Architects.)

The following are two examples of their work: Bassetti's Henry M. Jackson Building in Seattle (right) and Belluschi's Portland Art Museum in Portland (below). (Right, courtesy Joe Mabel; below, courtesy M.O. Stevens.)

Born near Genoa, Charles "Cash" Guinasso immigrated in 1919 with his family to America, joining his father, who was already in San Francisco. In 1928, the fishnet weaving company Cash worked at was bought out by a Seattle company, and when offered a job to work for the new company, he accepted and moved to Seattle. He managed a rigging crew in a net loft for Pacific Marine Supply for many years. His work had a stellar reputation among fishermen along the West Coast, including the men of the Alaska cannery fleet. He was so in demand that even the Fisheries Research Institute called on him for advice on specialized net production. (Both, courtesy Gerard Guinasso.)

With the help of his growing family, Cash went into the fishing gear business to make extra money, and some of his boys, and his daughter, too, were just as fast as Cash with a needle. Cash's design skills stretched to wire knotting, going so far as inventing a collapsible crab pot—a boon to many crab and sports fishermen. Whenever someone would ask him how he would like to be paid, he would say, "Cash," hence his nickname. Cash had many friends, including his priest, Fr. Gerard Evoy, pastor of Our Lady of Mount Virgin, who would come to hang out and watch him in his workshop, affectionately known as "the Shack." (Both, courtesy Gerard Guinasso.)

An impoverished marquis turned renowned fashion designer from a distinguished Florentine family, Emilio Pucci traded his skiing skills for an education at Reed College, Portland. He designed the school's first ski team uniform and served as its ski master. (Courtesy author's collection.)

Portland mayor Earl Riley (right) is seen conferring with New York mayor Fiorello La Guardia (left), then President Roosevelt's national director of civilian defense, on La Guardia's 60th birthday in 1937. The mayors were both in Los Angeles, where Mayor La Guardia was presiding over the Pacific Coast Regional Conference of Mayors. The Pacific Northwest was still heavily beset by economic depression, and unemployment relief was a focal topic at the conference. (Courtesy Portland Municipal Archives.)

City of Portland (OR) Archives, A2010-019.91

Dr. Henry Suzzallo, with Italian-Croatian roots, had first served as an educator at the prestigious Stanford and Columbia Universities before becoming University of Washington president (1915–1926). During his administration, he envisioned a library that was to be the "soul of the university." Italian sculptures of Leonardo da Vinci, Galileo, and Dante line the interior of the library, which was named in his honor after his death. (Both, courtesy author's collection.)

IN HONOR OF HENRY SUZZALLO
DISTINGUISHED EDUCATOR AND PRESIDENT
OF THE UNIVERSITY FROM 1915 TO 1926
WHO SET THE PATTERN FOR THE DEVELOPMENT
OF THE UNIVERSITY INTO ONE OF THE OUTSTANDING
INSTITUTIONS OF HIGHER EDUCATION IN THE NATION
THIS BUILDING WAS NAMED
HENRY SUZZALLO LIBRARY
BY THE BOARD OF REGENTS SEPTEMBER 3 1948

After speaking at the University of Washington's centennial year celebration in 1961, President John F. Kennedy rode with Sen. Warren Magnuson (middle) and Gov. Albert Rosellini (far right) in a parade in downtown Seattle. (Courtesy Museum of History and Industry.)

Albert Rosellini, from Tacoma, was governor from 1957 to 1965. During a visit to the Seattle's World's Fair in 1962, Elvis presented the governor (left) with a prosciutto leg, allegedly from Elvis's father's hog farm. (Courtesy Museum of History and Industry.)

Seven

AT SPORTS

Italians extended their fun into playing sports, including bocce—the sport most associated with their culture. Some ventured into sports where Italians were not previously well known, like weight lifting, bowling, boxing, and racing, be they cars or hydroplanes. Wrestling was a sport where Oregon's own Ernie Piluso battled Pete Belcastro for the Pacific Coast Light Heavyweight Title in 1940. Baseball was one sport where Italians Edo Vanni and Ron Santo of Seattle dominated.

But before there were any team sports in the Seattle area, there was car racing. Prominent racing legends Gene Romano and Mario Bianchi dominated at the Salem and Eugene fairgrounds in Oregon and at the Silver Lake and Yakima Speedways in Washington, respectively. From 1918 to 1941, Mario's racing wins were recorded and followed with much vigor. The accomplishments of both men were lauded in regular, as well as racing, newspapers and magazines until Gene bowed out in 1924. Mario continued setting stock records, including one in 1932 that was not broken for a quarter century! He even ran advertisements for his auto repair company with him in his trademark clean uniform, shirt, and tie sitting in his famous No. 38 race car.

The 1952 Olympics saw Al Rossi, coxswain for the US four-man crew rowing team, head to Helsinki and score a bronze medal for the University of Washington, narrowly missing out on the silver medal. Though not the same team, the University of Washington again was in the news at the 1936 Olympics in Berlin when they narrowly beat out Italy and Germany to win the gold medal—right under Hitler's nose.

Inspired by strongmen of the time, Clevio Massimo and Angelo "Charles Atlas" Siciliano, the Loprinzi family of Portland built their own weights with concrete poured into empty cans and a pipe in between. In the 1920s and 1930s, bodybuilding was a fringe pursuit, its practitioners consigned to sideshows at circuses. The 10 Loprinzi brothers' success proved otherwise. Outgrowing their makeshift home gym in 1930, they opened their own club, which is still in use today.

The 1930s was a major turning point in America for female athletes. Physical education and recreational activities for women at high schools, colleges, and post-college were ramping up. In the Pacific Northwest, hiking, tennis, skiing, swimming, golf, and sailing were all sports that saw women's participation increase. Born in 1950, Lynn Colella of Seattle, Washington, was part of the University of Washington team and represented the United States at the 1972 Olympics in Munich, where she won the silver medal in the 200-meter butterfly. She was also a two-time Pan American Games gold medalist, 10-time national champion, and ranked No. 1 in the world in the 200-meter butterfly.

Mario Bianchi loved working on cars and had his own shop in Seattle for years. From 1918 to 1941, he loved driving cars, too—especially at high speeds and on tracks. Note the spectators in the trees (below) at the Tacoma Speedway. (Both, courtesy John Bianchi.)

He won the first race he ever drove in Coeur d'Alene, winning both prize and lap money. He was the Northwest champion from 1931 to 1932. Note the man holding up the prize cup behind Mario (below). (Both, courtesy John Bianchi.)

Italian men in Garlic Gulch (Seattle) often played bocce together in open fields or someone's backyard. On April 19, 1946, the players were, from left to right (first row): Nicheolangelo Recchia, Giuseppe Vacca, Chi-Chi Genzale, Salvatore Yazzolino, Antonio D'Ambrosio, and Nick Pandon; (second row) Genaro Genzale. (Courtesy Donna Workman.)

John Ursino played baseball for the Italian Club, Franklin High School, and even semipro for a farm team after playing for his alma mater, Seattle University. Later, he played on Boeing's team in Seattle in the 1950s. (Courtesy Lisa Ursino.)

In the 1930s–1940s, the Loprinzi brothers were physical fitness stars before that was a thing. Phil was a football star at the University of Portland. Gus, a 1930 Olympic hopeful, had a genius way with metalwork and welded the family's first equipment before they branched out into owning their own gym. Joe was inducted into the Oregon Sports Hall of Fame in 1991. From left to right are cousins Pedro and Frank Greco, cousin "Doc" Loprinzi, cousin Moe Loprinzi, Joe Loprinzi, Sam Loprinzi, cousin Dave Loprinzi, cousin Tony Loprinzi, Phil Loprinzi, and cousin George Pavlich. In 1935, Sam (middle), together with Al Howland (top) and George Pavlich (bottom), performed as acrobats in The La Prinzi Trio-Athletic Artistry. (Both, courtesy the Loprinzi family.)

Baseball star Edo Vanni (right) and hall-of-famer Ron Santo (left) were both from Seattle, though Ron played in Chicago. Between the two of them, their careers spanned the gamut from player to coach, general manager, broadcaster, and ultimately, goodwill ambassadors for teams that, at times, could use all the help they could muster. (Both, courtesy Chris Alfieri.)

Eight

AT PLAY

In the first half of the 20th century, immigrant life was not all toil and troubles. Italian families had fun, too, even if all they could afford was an afternoon at the beach after Mass with a picnic nearby. If there was a little extra in their pocket that week, they might enjoy a *sorbetto* or gelato for a penny or a nickel, depending on the decade and if a peddler was nearby.

Often, music was involved, especially in large gatherings. Mandolins, violins, *tamburelli*, and accordions were ubiquitous. The repertoire ranged from popular Italian folk ballads, war tunes, and songs of propaganda and protest to ethnic laments, arias, hymns, and the tarantella—all of which were played, sung, or danced to.

Italians in the Pacific Northwest branched out of singing with their families and at church to forming professional bands to play supper clubs, dance halls, and on the stage and silver screen, too. Some made it into the recording studio with big band sounds, jazz, and opera. Marching bands and orchestras traveled the national circuit and often performed at exhibitions, including the major fairs in the area, like the Northwestern Industrial Exhibition of Spokane Falls (1890), the Lewis and Clark Centennial Exposition in Portland (1905), and the Alaska-Yukon-Pacific Exposition in Seattle (1909).

Vaudeville was popular entertainment in the Northwest. In the early 1900s, jokes at the expense of women or someone's national heritage and ethnicity were a staple not only of vaudeville but also American life. By the end of vaudeville's heyday in the early 1930s, most ethnic acts had been eliminated from the bill or toned down to be less offensive. However, ethnic caricatures continued to thrive in radio programs, such as *Life with Luigi*. Though it was liberally peppered with stereotypes, it helped to erase reasons of distrust of postwar Italians and balance out the shame imparted to many Italian Americans as they identified with Luigi's intelligence and integrity.

In the 1930s, the Gondoliers played accordion, violin, saxophone, and clarinet in vaudeville and Pantages theaters up and down the West Coast. Together with other Seattle-area musicians, the Gondoliers even accompanied the famous Chef Joseph Milani of Los Angeles, who toured his "The Singing Chef Cooking School" in sold-out music halls singing arias as he taught housewives everywhere how to cook Italian economically.

Later, bandleader and Seattle musical institution Frank Sugia and his trio dressed in Victorian costume to perform as the Strolling Minstrels at the Frederick & Nelson department store. The trio were invited to entertain at Seafair galas and on the buses Vito's Restaurant chartered to attend Husky football games and to accompany the big names of Frank Sinatra, Dean Martin, Bing Crosby, and Bob Hope.

Sponsored by the Order of the Sons of Italy, Sylvia Croce was chosen to represent the Italian community at the 1950 Seafair in Seattle. (Courtesy Sylvia Croce Zappoli.)

Italians from different regions came together for the first time in Seattle when the community worked as one to participate in Italian Day as part of the 1909 Alaska-Yukon-Pacific Exposition. (Courtesy Chris Alfieri.)

In Washington in 1938, Italians loved participating in parades, evidenced by spectacularly decorated ones at the Daffodil Parade in Tacoma (above) and at the Auburn Day Parade (below). (Above, courtesy Washington State Historical Society; below, courtesy White River Valley Museum.)

JOHNNY CASH   SUN Recording
                   Artist

Personal Management
BOB NEAL
Suite 1916, Sterick Bldg. Memphis, Tenn.

Charles Ceciliani wanted a dance hall. His wife, Adoline, wanted a trailer court. In the end, they opened the Division Street Corral in Portland in 1948. They bought 10 acres and took two years to build it. Their four children, Art, Joanna, Jeannie, and Carl, helped out behind the bar, checked coats, swept floors, and cleaned up the parking. For decades, The "D Street Corral," as it was known, was a dance hall that hosted big-name acts like Minnie Pearl, Johnny Cash, Buck Owens, Tex Williams, Bobby Vee, The Kingsmen, Paul Revere & the Raiders, Ike and Tina Turner, Roy Orbison, Bobby Darin, and Count Basie. A poster of Johnny Cash playing at the venue sold online for $20,000. The Corral was demolished in 2007. (Both, courtesy Joanna Ceciliani.)

George Amato enjoyed sharing entertainment with others, whether it was a bowling alley or a supper club. He owned and operated several supper clubs from the 1940s to the 1960s in Astoria; Vancouver, British Columbia; and Portland. He brought in top talent like Sophie Tucker, Ella Fitzgerald, West Point Glee Club, and Sammy Davis Jr., and Amato's Supper Club became the hottest nightspot in Portland. (Both, courtesy Georgene Raab.)

SOUVENIR FROM
AMATO'S SUPPER CLUB
Palace of the Pacific
ASTORIA, OREGON

Lola Sugia began her singing career in the 1940s. She could hold her own in big bands, swing orchestras, and at supper clubs in Seattle and Portland as well as in the recording studio. Today, her daughter Maia Santell carries on the tradition in her inimitable blues and jazz style, plus forays into Latin and rock while playing cruises, festivals, weddings, and private and corporate parties. (Courtesy Maia Santell.)

In April 1952, a group of Italian ladies in the Renton Hill neighborhood made it a point to celebrate one another's birthdays and formed a club to solidify their commitment to party on a regular basis. (Courtesy No. 1989.055.2792, Renton History Museum.)

Josephine Vitarelli performed at the Orpheum Theatre in Seattle at 19 years old. For years later, she entertained at weddings and other celebratory events, playing favorites like "La Luna'messo Mare," the wedding song from *The Godfather* movie. Her son Joe said he would dance to her tarantella until his legs became rubbery. Her blue-collar worker husband, John, and grandfather Giovanni loved when she played "Hallelujah, I'm a Bum." (Courtesy Joe Zavaglia.)

For several decades, Sylvia Croce taught the children of American servicemen at schools on military bases in Germany, Japan, and Italy. During one vacation in 1950s Spain, while watching the running of bulls in Pamplona, she met Ernest Hemingway. (Courtesy Sylvia Croce Zappoli.)

Carlo Petosa and Vittore Giardinieri ("Victor Gardener") were two musical instrument pioneers in the Pacific Northwest. The first lived in Seattle and the second in Grants Pass, Oregon. Both men crafted their instruments by hand, *uno alla volta*, and both grew up desperately wanting their own accordion and violin, respectively. As life would have it, they much preferred the manufacturing to the playing of them. Carlo started in 1922 traversing the country on the vaudeville circuit before choosing to settle in Seattle. He meticulously measured, cut, and honed one-of-a-kind accordions beloved the world over—now built by the fourth generation of Petosas. Victor was second generation and mostly stayed in place, learning to craft violins, violas, and cellos, totaling 405 instruments in 96 years. He was unique in that he found, harvested, milled, and cured his own wood from unharvested trees, and he often gave away his creations to needy local students. (Left, courtesy Joe Petosa Jr.; below, courtesy Lake Creek Historical Society.)

Vito Lanza immigrated to Tacoma from Sicily. He was a retired truck driver with various construction companies and a World War I vet, and he volunteered with the Salvation Army. He had a deep appreciation for his good fortune in America, and he loved displaying various mementos of his patriotism in a special room in his home. (Courtesy Tacoma Public Library, General Photograph Collection.)

Italians have a deep love of family, and none more so than between a grandparent and a grandchild. Joe Salle and his grandfather Giuseppe Salle had a particularly close bond, and they loved spending time together. Here, they are in *nonno*'s backyard next to a fountain Giuseppe built. (Courtesy Joe Salle.)

Typical for many Italian homes is a cantina, where "dago" wine is often made and cellared, preserved food is stored, and meals are enjoyed, like this one in Frank Buono's home. Derogatory names like "wop" and "dago" were ethnic slurs hurled at Italians during the mass migration years, and for many years after, but some Italians have repurposed "dago," like Tony Bacino, who prints Dago Wine labels for his stock. (Above, courtesy Frank Buono; below, courtesy Tony Bacino.)

Nine

POST 1950

By 1950, Italian pioneers had lived through the formation of labor unions (a few specifically benefitting women), World War I, the Spanish flu, the advent of movies and radio, the stock market crash of 1929, the Great Depression, Roosevelt's New Deal, the attack on Pearl Harbor, World War II, and the Soviet-backed army of North Korea invading South Korea. Amidst a relatively calm political and socioeconomic climate, midcentury America was a time of prosperity for many, including Italians.

They had moved out of their initial clapboard settlements and cheap lodging houses and into Craftsman-style abodes in cities and suburbs. Several old city neighborhoods experienced displacement when new developments were needed like in Spokane's Hillyard area or when highways paved over farms, businesses, and homes in South Portland's Marquam Gulch and Seattle's Rainier Valley. Once-thriving company towns in Idaho and Washington are just a shell of what they once were, and some now do not even exist on a map.

With the success of their ancestors' activism with labor unions and civil rights, the next generation attended post-secondary education in droves. Some pursued careers in law, social justice, and politics—locally and regionally. Still others lent their talents to the fields of sports, science, and the musical and literary arts. The professional classes, like architecture, medicine, engineering, and the like, drew interest, too. Quite a few went on to expand their initial family businesses or start new ones including restaurants and grocery stores—the hub of the community then and now.

A few of the once-vibrant shops and restaurants found in Little Italys all over the Pacific Northwest have joined a ghost fleet of lost Italian businesses that helped define a proud heritage. Businesses, like towns, do sometimes disappear, yet many experience a resurgence as the descendants of pioneers embrace their roots in an effort to recapture the nostalgia of the parents' and grandparents' day. They may not be able to replace the historical bits, but new ideas pop up all the time, because the future is not dim, just transformed, even if incrementally.

Over a century ago, the forefathers and foremothers of present-day Italian Americans left their small known world for a vast unknown one. Their motto could easily have been the following: *Per aspera ad astra*, "through hardship, to the stars." Some days, their fear overtook their courage, but more often than not, their courage won. It is that found courage to imagine a new life—in the thoughts and customs of a new country alongside the social and domestic remnants of the old country—that was the foundational inspiration for this book. The past, coexisting with the present, provides people today with the experience to hope for the future.

Just as some celebrities were known by one name, so was the legend known as "Pelle"—a master gardener, *buongustaio*, wine expert, sought-after lecturer, renowned teacher, respected author, and generous philanthropist. Angelo Pellegrini, together with his family, immigrated from Casabianca in Tuscany as a boy in 1913, settling in Grays Harbor, Washington. As an adult, he made his mark as an English professor with a paesano's heart at the University of Washington, and as an author, publishing definitive works about Italian culture, food, and wine. A culinary patriarch, he wrote gastronomic books, such as *The Unprejudiced Palate, An Immigrant's Quest, An American Dream,* and *The Food-Lover's Garden,* that went on to influence many prominent chefs and food writers. He has the unique privilege of having a pole bean, the Pellegrini bean, named after him. (Courtesy Isernio family.)

Inspired by his mother's recipes, one-time pipefitter Frank Isernio Jr. turned a hobby and entrepreneurial grit into an innovative sausage manufacturing company, winning awards across the country and the world. As a pioneer family, Frank's parents farmed the land where Boeing Field now stands, which helped birth Seattle's Pike Place Market. From humble beginnings, his vision of uncompromising quality and serving his Italian community run deep. (Courtesy Isernio family.)

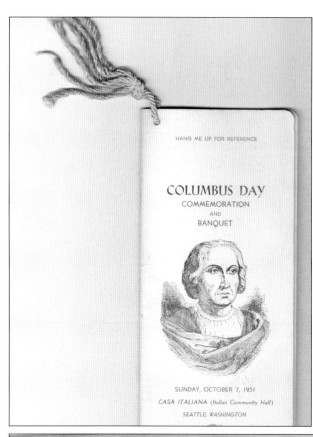

Every year, Columbus Day in the United States is celebrated by all Italian Americans, often with annual banquets, which, at Seattle's Casa Italiana in 1951, included a program that many paesanos contributed to with good wishes to the community hosting the event. After World War I, there were early efforts by some Italian clubs to have mayors declare an Italy America Day. (Left, courtesy Joe Salle; below, courtesy Portland Municipal Archives.)

Italian immigration to the Americas had a second wave after World War II. The Bessich family was one such example. Bruno joined the Italian Navy during the war, and afterward, he worked as a policeman in Trieste, training dogs for the force. In 1956, escaping Yugoslavian president Josip Tito's Communist regime, Bruno; his wife, Rosa; and daughter Flavia sailed on the *General Langfitt* for New York City. After the war, many ships were reacquired by the Navy for new assignments. In 1950, the *Langfitt* was retrofitted as an overseas transport carrying troops, dependents, and even European refugees to the United States under the Refugees Relief Act. The Bessich family immigrated to Portland to make a better life. Bruno worked hard to provide for his family. His favorite pastime was dancing, and he enjoyed whirling Rosa around at every opportunity. (Both, courtesy Flavia Bessich.)

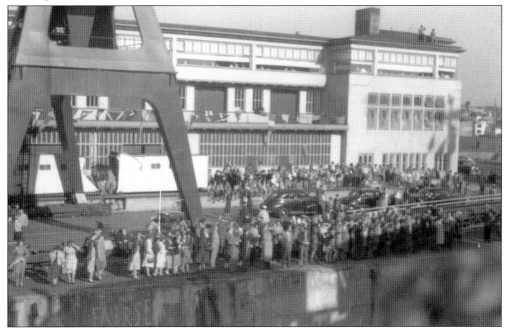

Roberto Tacchi was another example of a late immigrant. A seventh-generation Florentine woodcarver, Roberto landed in Seattle in 1963. His woodwork was popular and can been seen at various chapels, the front doors for the Seattle Yacht Club, the interior of the King of Thailand's Boeing 747, and a torah crown for a Mercer Island synagogue. Local Italians and non-Italians treasure his highly prized seashells and carved frames in their homes. (Both, courtesy Chris Alfieri.)

Roberto Tacchi's masterpiece (not shown) was a stunning Late Gothic altar and triptych to display Leonardo da Vinci's *Salvator Mundi* painting (c. 1512) for the Henry Art Gallery. It is a fitting tribute then that the label "Renaissance man" was applied to Roberto, as his talents extended to cooking, conversation, music, history, and literature. Roberto passed away on May 15, 2019, at the age of 80. His energy and passion for life were unequaled and are sorely missed by so many. (Both, courtesy Chris Alfieri.)

Discover Thousands of Local History Books
Featuring Millions of Vintage Images

Arcadia Publishing, the leading local history publisher in the United States, is committed to making history accessible and meaningful through publishing books that celebrate and preserve the heritage of America's people and places.

Find more books like this at
www.arcadiapublishing.com

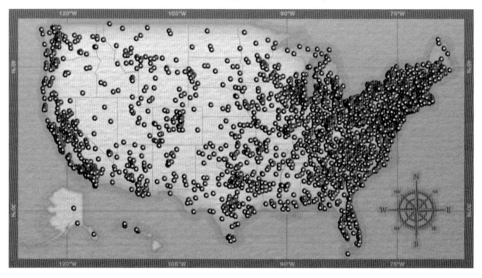

Search for your hometown history, your old stomping grounds, and even your favorite sports team.

Consistent with our mission to preserve history on a local level, this book was printed in South Carolina on American-made paper and manufactured entirely in the United States. Products carrying the accredited Forest Stewardship Council (FSC) label are printed on 100 percent FSC-certified paper.

MADE IN THE
USA